# Amazing ways to Monetize
# YOUR SKILLS

Turn What You Know into Profit with Practical Strategies for Success through Online Business.

Jack Patrick

Amazing ways to Monetize Your Skills: Turn What You Know into Profit with Practical Strategies for Success
© 2024 [**Jack Patrick**]

All rights reserved. No part of this book may be reproduced, distributed, or transmitted in any form or by any means, including photocopying, recording, or other electronic or mechanical methods, without the prior written permission of the publisher, except in the case of brief quotations embodied in critical reviews and certain other noncommercial uses permitted by copyright law.

Publisher's Note: The author and publisher have made every effort to ensure that the information in this book was correct at the time of publication. The author and publisher do not assume and hereby disclaim any liability to any party for any loss, damage, or disruption caused by errors or omissions, whether such errors or omissions result from negligence, accident, or any other cause.

## TABLE OF CONTENTS

**INTRODUCTION** ......................................................... **10**
    "Why to Monetize Your Skills" ........................... 10
    Your Path to Creating an Online Business ..... 10
    What's inside? ........................................................ 11

**CHAPTER 1** .................................................................. **14**
**IDENTIFYING YOUR UNIQUE SKILLS** ................. **14**
    Here are six tips to help you determine your unique ability: ........................................................ 15
    Converting Passion Into A Marketable Product .................................................................. 17
    Real-Life Stories: Finding Your Niche ............. 20

**CHAPTER 2:** ................................................................. **24**
**ESTABLISHING YOUR ONLINE PRESENCE— A PROFESSIONAL WEBSITE** .................................... **24**
    The importance of social media ...................... 39
    Success Stories: Building an Online Brand .... 42
    AMAZON ................................................................. 42
    STARBUCKS ........................................................... 45
    NOKIA ...................................................................... 47
    3M ............................................................................. 47
    AVON ....................................................................... 49

**CHAPTER 3:** ................................................................. **50**
**OVERCOMING COMMON CHALLENGES - ADDRESSING SELF-DOUBT** ................................... **50**

Managing Your Time Effectively......................55
Personal Story: Overcoming Obstacles..........69
There are four factors that can keep you from being interested, and I believe they will keep you from succeeding.........................................72

## CHAPTER 4:................................................................74
## MARKET YOUR SKILLS.............................................74

Effective Social Media Strategies.....................74
Using Email Marketing To Engage Customers..79
Entrepreneur Insights: Successful Marketing Tactics.............................................................94

## CHAPTER 5:................................................................98
## MONETIZING YOUR KNOWLEDGE - EARNING MONEY ONLINE........................................................98

20 Ways to Earn Money from Home...............98
Price Your Products and Services.................107
Real-World Examples: Converting Knowledge into Income..................................................117

## CHAPTER 6:..............................................................120
## CREATING VALUABLE CONTENT........................120

Writing Blogs, Articles, and E-books.............120
Producing Engaging Videos and Webinars..162
7 Tips for Making Engaging Videos................163
Expert Tips: Content that Engages Your

Audience ............................................................. 173

**CHAPTER 7:** ...................................................... **176**
**BUILDING A LOYAL COMMUNITY To GROW YOUR AUDIENCE** ..................................... **178**

Excellent customer service practices ........... 182

Stories from the Field: Engaging Your Audience ............................................................ 185

**CHAPTER 8:** ...................................................... **185**
**SCALING YOUR BUSINESS: AND OUTSOURCING** ................................................ **188**

Using Technology for Growth ........................ 193

Entrepreneur Journeys: Successful Scaling Up ........................................................................ 201

**CHAPTER 9:** ..................................................... **206**
**MAINTAINING LONG-TERM SUCCESS BY STAYING CURRENT WITH INDUSTRY TRENDS. 208**

Continuous Learning and Improvement ....... 211

Personal Accounts: Staying ahead and innovating ........................................................... 221

**Conclusion:** ..................................................... **223**
**Your Roadmap to Success** ........................... **223**

# INTRODUCTION

Thanks for visiting "Amazing ways to Monetize Your Skills: Turn What You Know into Profit with Practical Strategies for Success through Online Business". This book is a step-by-step approach to turning your knowledge into a successful internet business. Whether you're just getting started or looking to advance, you'll discover insights, tales, and guidance to guide you every step of the way.

## "Why to Monetize Your Skills"

Everyone is good at something, whether from experience or enthusiasm. This book will teach you how to apply what you know to start a business. When you share your skills and expertise, you add value that others will pay for.

## Your Path to Creating an Online Business

Starting an online business may seem difficult, but it does not have to be. This book breaks things down into simple steps to help you start

and expand your business. You will learn how to identify and market your unique skills.
- Overcome common issues such as self-doubt and time management.
- Establish a professional online presence through a website and social media.
- Market your expertise to acquire and retain consumers.
- Earn money in a variety of ways.
- Create useful material for your readers.
- Build and sustain your business to ensure long-term success.

## What's inside?

You'll read stories about successful entrepreneurs who started out like you. They share their experiences and lessons learnt, offering practical counsel. Each chapter focuses on a distinct aspect of starting an online business, from the first idea to long-term success.

You'll find actionable suggestions and techniques, such as content planning, email marketing setup, and customer feedback management. This book provides the tools you need to move forward with confidence.

**Let us get started.**

Are you ready to leverage your skills to start an internet business? You are not alone. Many entrepreneurs have been where you are now, and their tales will motivate and guide you. Let us dive in and start constructing your online empire together!

The initial step is the most crucial. Let's work together to develop your expertise into a successful internet business. Welcome to Amazing Ways to monetize Your Skills.

# CHAPTER 1

# IDENTIFYING YOUR UNIQUE SKILLS

How to Identify Your Unique Ability:
Each of us is unique in our experiences, skill set, and what energizes and motivates us. But it's remarkable how many of us underestimate this since we've never learnt to recognize, let alone appreciate, our unique skills.

This is why I encourage everyone to try the Unique Ability Discovery Process, which reveals the ways you naturally strive and draws attention to the things that motivate and fulfill you, allowing you to better comprehend your effect.

Identifying your Unique Ability and placing language around it so you can communicate your "why" isn't always easy; it takes digging deeper.

And, frequently, the things we excel at are so deeply established in us that we fail to identify them as unique or special. However, if your goal is to take control and create the life you want, Unique Ability is a surefire way to get there.

## Here are six tips to help you determine your unique ability:

- You enjoy doing this in a variety of settings, including business. Your Unique Ability is a combo of what you're very skilled at and have a strong love for. But don't limit yourself to thinking about it only in terms of employment.
Push yourself beyond that and consider how you add value at home, at school, and with family and friends. Unique Ability isn't just how you make money; it could also be what your family looks to you for.
It shines in a variety of settings and opportunities. Look for and focus on the activities and behaviors that come naturally to you and stand out in a variety of contexts.
- Your Unique Ability is the essence you bring to all situations in which you thrive, and it likely comes so naturally to you that others will realize it before you do.
- Your Unique Ability is "factory installed"; you've been doing it since you were a

child. To some extent, you've done things this way since you were a child. Consult your parents, siblings, teachers, or anyone who knew you when you were younger for advice.

- Consider how you contributed or were recognized when you were much younger.

   It comes so readily that you may not recognize it as anything exceptional. We tend to take our Unique Ability for granted because we've always done it this way.

   It might not seem flashy or intriguing. It may even appear mundane because we're so used to being ourselves and doing things this way. However, when you notice how you naturally strive, you get closer to understanding what motivates you.

- Other people rely on you for these unique abilities. What do other people always rely on you for? Look for clues to help you find your Unique Ability.

   You can practice this for a lifetime and still find it fascinating. Understanding and honing your unique ability is a life-long endeavor. The more you use it, the sharper it becomes and the better you understand its impact.

So use it and see it evolve to help you become the best version of yourself, as well as discover new ways to add your own unique worth.

- Discovering your own abilities is a key to achieving ultimate independence. It will never seem like work, and it will allow you to see how and where you can have the most influence.

Use these signs to obtain a better knowledge of why you do what you do, allowing you to be more thoughtful about it. Identifying your role and influence is one of the most satisfying things you can do for yourself—and people around you.

## Converting Passion Into A Marketable Product

It is beneficial to turn your passion into a business because it will be less expensive and more convenient for you to start.

However, there are a few things you should consider before investing time in launching a business based on your passion.
- Check the marketability.

It would be beneficial if you spent a significant amount of time developing that into a business, but first, determine whether your passion has a market. Did you learn about the people in your circle's requirements and the answers they seek for their problems? If that's the case, determine whether the product you create as a pastime will meet their demands.
- Identify your target market.

That means the geographical area in which your clients dwell if you can reach them, conduct a survey, and explain your product, particularly the benefits they would derive from it.
- Check your competitor.

This is to ensure their marketing strategies, consumers, and suppliers; even if you are utilizing your pastime to start a business, you may need the supplier to stock up on fresh products to generate a saleable product. As a result, you must monitor your competition, but doing so can land you in serious difficulty; if you

try to replicate their ways, you will learn and build some alternatives to apply to your firm.
- Pricing.

How are you going to price your product? Do you have any ideas on how to price it? Remember that if you price it too high, you will not sell, and if you lower the price, you will sell more, but you may end up losing money because you did not account for the expenses of starting the business.
- Location.

Starting a business from home will be a safe way to keep expenses low.

So, everything depends on the market you'll service; if you're still seeking for the suitable clients, what you sell will land you in hot water, so you can advertise your goods offline instead. However, you must utilize free marketing methods to promote your goods, and if you want to spend money on commercials, you may face serious consequences.

To be successful in business, you must plan ahead of time, be dedicated, and work consistently. You'll be enthusiastic about this business because it's your pastime. If you lose passion at any time, you will get into difficulty and lose everything you have.

## Real-Life Stories: Finding Your Niche

Here are a few stories to help you discover your niche: I've spent my entire life hunting for a "niche." A niche where I can establish a successful career. A niche that naturally occurs to me. But it was quite difficult to find. I tried literally everything in the book! They advised you to ask your parents what activities you enjoyed as a child. And my parents would respond, "You only liked to play hide-and-seek and watch Oswald and Noddy." I had no notion how to discover my passion from this. They said to find out what extracurricular activities you were most active in while in school. But "studying hard" was all I did in school. My parents, like all competitive parents in India, desired good marks. They did not want me to "waste" my time on other activities because it would interfere with my schoolwork. So I usually stayed away. They advised you to identify the types of things you typically purchase and have a little "more" information about them than others. But the only items I purchased were chips and cold drinks. That, too, I never wanted to know more about. They advised me to figure out what kind of information I consume the most frequently. But all I saw were training videos for my tests and motivational films to help me cope with exam anxiety. I was so frustrated all the time. How could I ever find my niche? That was when I gave up. I began doing everything for everyone. I would do graphic design, video editing, content authoring, UI and UX design, ad campaigns, copywriting, website development, and whatever else the client requested. I did that for one long year. Yes, this was difficult. But I had to investigate. I didn't want to settle for a job I wasn't passionate about. That one year, from May 2020 to March 2021, was the most crazy yet enjoyable year of my life. Every day was an adventure. As soon as I woke up, the world began throwing challenges at me, as if the cosmos were saying, "Show me how you'll handle this one, huh." After gaining practical experience in nearly all of these sectors, I had a clearer understanding of what I disliked and what I enjoyed doing. It provided me with the clarity I had been seeking. Now, it's not like I've still figured out my niche. But my list is far shorter (copywriting and email marketing), and I'm happier doing what I enjoy every day to earn money. You know, sometimes you don't have many options. Sometimes the only option is to brute-force your interest down. Taking a year off to just explore and figure out what you do better than others is quite crucial. As the saying goes, contentment comes not from money but from knowing you're doing something your heart and soul were meant to do. I'd love to know what you think of this.

# CHAPTER 2:

# ESTABLISHING YOUR ONLINE PRESENCE— A PROFESSIONAL WEBSITE

How to Build a Professional Website
- Strategize your brand.
- Master the web design.
- Prioritize website usability.
- Optimize for Search Engines
- Professionalize your website. Optimize for mobile.
- Create a content marketing plan.
- Maintain your professional website.

- **Strategize your brand:** Begin by creating a clear and consistent brand strategy that will influence every aspect of your website, from the general objective to the guiding visual philosophy and tone of voice. All of this should become obvious as you investigate the following: Identify your target market. Who are they? What demographic groups do they belong to? What do they prefer to do? How does your target audience see themselves? How will your business or website impact their lives? Research your competitors: Conduct some market research to gain a sense of what the competition is doing, their strengths and shortcomings, and how you might carve out a space for yourself in the area. Define your brand's identity: How would you characterize your brand in three words? What is the vision that drives your brand? Consider your brand's identity and identify concrete characteristics such as brand colors, lexicon, and style. Prepare consistent branding materials. Now it's time to get practical and create the elements that will soon appear on your website and other branding assets. Make sure to design your own logo, graphics, slogans, videos, written content, and more. These pieces should all be consistent with your brand identity and have a purpose in your branding strategy.

- **Master web design:** From selecting the proper website color scheme to creating the perfect layout for your site, there are numerous factors of professional website design to consider. If you know how to design a website from scratch and have some past expertise, you may start by selecting a blank website template and determining whether to create a static or dynamic website. If you're concerned about how long it takes to make a website and want to save time, you may create a great website with Wix's HTML website creator in the three steps below: Select a template or start with AI: When you use a website builder utilizing What You See Is What You Get (WYSIWYG) software, such as Wix, you don't need to write any code—it's all built into the UI. Customers can use the platform's customizable website templates to build their own sites from the ground up. There is a large collection of professional website templates for various themes, styles, and objectives. Find the template that best fits your concept, whether you're building a personal website, an online store, or another form of site. Ideally, the one you choose will be pre-structured to meet your requirements and align with your business objectives. Alternatively, you may have Wix's AI website maker create your site for you and then edit it later. This means that you don't have to be fluent in HTML, CSS, or other web development terminology. Simply interact with AI and allow Wix's artificial design intelligence to do its magic. Discover more about how to build a website with AI. If you're an expert, Wix Studio offers capabilities like responsive AI and a web production platform designed for agencies. Customize your template: Now is the time to personalize and change it to create your own website. Add all of your stuff, including text, videos, links, and photographs. Wix suggests utilizing JPEG, PNG, and GIF files for photos to ensure they look great on your site. Next, use the editor's site and theme design to ensure that your site design is consistent with your brand. Customization can be as simple or complex as you wish. For ideas, check out this collection of eye-catching Wix websites made from three different templates. Take note of how the original simple website templates have been modified to create one-of-a-kind, custom-designed websites. Tweak the appearance: There is much more to making a website than simply selecting the best fonts, colors, and photos. You can use a range of media elements to improve your overall appearance. Try including background films or animation into your website design to provide movement, or use parallax scrolling to create a sense of depth.

- **Prioritize website usability**: Your website must capture the attention of any potential consumer, but in order to keep people exploring, you must also give a great user experience. A gorgeous website that does not work correctly will not take you far. When creating a professional website, pay attention to these crucial factors. For optimal website navigation, ensure that the site structure is clear and intuitive. Visitors should be able to simply browse between pages and subpages via the main menu or internal links. Content Hierarchy: Hierarchy is one of the seven design concepts; thus, it deserves special consideration. Your goal is to direct users through your website in the sequence that best meets your interests. When considering how to design a website, ensure that the most important layout aspects are noticeable. Reflect this hierarchy in your design by emphasizing the most important items using size, color, and positioning on the page. For example, if you want users to subscribe to your service, make sure the 'Subscribe' button is prominent on the website. This landing page showing how to establish a blog with a blog builder exemplifies proper content hierarchy, complete with huge headings and eye-catching buttons. Calls-to-action (CTAs) are short statements that encourage site users to take direct action. They can prompt visitors to "Register Free," "Get Yours Today," or "Subscribe." In short, they tell visitors exactly what you want them to do and make it simple for them to believe what happens once they click a button. Readability is a fundamental principle of typography. Use clear typefaces and comfortable font sizes, make sure your text colors contrast effectively with the backdrop colors, and provide enough of empty space (whitespace) around your written content. Check out our guide for additional information on how to make a website accessible. The website footer is the bottom section of your site (the header is at the top). Footers are not immediately visible to site visitors, but they can be used in a variety of ways to improve usability. Consider providing your contact information at the bottom, along with links to your social media outlets and privacy policy. You might also include a simplified site map with links to all of your pages as well as a brief introduction to yourself or a site disclaimer.

- **Optimize for search engines:** Getting your website to rank highly in search results is one of the most effective strategies to attract traffic. This is why it's critical to focus search engine optimization (SEO) in the early phases of developing a professional website. SEO, which is an important aspect of web marketing, is a science in and of itself. Its main elements are: Keyword Research: Put yourself in the position of your potential website visitor or customer. Which queries or phrases would people search for on Google to find your website? The keywords in their search queries can help you plan your SEO approach. Using keyword research tools, you may make an informed decision about which keywords to target. This might also help you choose a domain name that is relevant and searchable. Text: Every piece of text on your website, including your menu, FAQ page, blog, footer, and bio section, should be created with SEO in mind. While there are several SEO techniques to help your website, the overall goal is to discover subtle and elegant ways to include your keywords into your site's textual content without sacrificing quality. Search engine crawlers are intelligent, and they may downrank you if they believe you sound too much like an advertisement. Meta tags: Search engines, such as Google, scan your metadata. It is up to you to control what they view and how your site appears in search results. It is well worth taking the effort to add custom meta tags to your website in order to optimize your content and help search engines understand what your pages include.

Alt text: Images play an important role in your SEO efforts. Every image you post to your website should have alt text. Alt text is a brief sentence that tells search engines what the image portrays. As a result, your photographs can be 'discovered' in search results, which is why you should produce SEO-friendly alt text for all of your images.

connect building: In general, having other websites connect to your site will boost your ranking in search engine results. You may begin by submitting your professional website to directories, ensuring that all of your social media profiles link to it, and encouraging site users to share your material as well.

Keep in mind that SEO is a long-term effort that does not finish once your website is live. To obtain long-term outcomes, you will need to continually refine it.

- **Make your website more professional:** In addition to serving as the online face of your business or service, consider how your website might help you achieve even greater professional success. Depending on your company or field, your site may offer a variety of characteristics that will make it more appealing to your target market:

  Scheduling software is an excellent choice for organizing appointments online, as it allows you to take bookings and receive payments more easily while also showcasing your services in the best light.

**Online Store:** It has never been easier to develop and manage.

An eCommerce website with professional features such as advanced marketing tools, secure online payments, and several sales channels. You can construct your website from scratch or choose one of these online store templates.

**Fitness Website:** As you grow your fitness business, you'll need an all-in-one solution that includes gym management software, online booking and payments, and flexible staff and scheduling options.

Wix allows you to sell music straight on your website and keep 100% of the revenues. You'll also be able to grow your following while preserving complete creative independence.

**Essential apps:** The Wix App Market has a vast range of apps that will help you maximize the potential of your website. Consider using a tool to measure visitor metrics, a countdown timer to boost sales, and complex text animation to impress your visitors.

- **Optimize for mobile:** In today's world, it is critical to ensure that your website works equally well on mobile as it does on desktop. In reality, mobile usage statistics show that mobile devices account for more than half of web page views worldwide. Furthermore, since Google launched mobile-first indexing, websites are primarily prioritized in search results based on their mobile versions. Clearly, it is worthwhile to invest effort in optimizing your mobile website.
- When you build a professional website with Wix, the mobile editor immediately converts your desktop design into a mobile-friendly version. You can then modify the layout and style to fit mobile devices, giving special attention to readability, font sizing, and navigation. You can even turn your website into an app that users can download to their devices.

Wix Studio, a powerful creation platform designed specifically for designers and agencies, provides users with complete control over breakpoints. It has cutting-edge, responsive design as well as easy drag-and-drop functionality on a new, flexible canvas. This allows you complete design power, allowing you to develop your site for any viewport size.

- **Launch a content marketing plan:** Once your professional website is live, the primary difficulty changes to attracting and retaining visitors. You can prepare for this task by defining a content marketing plan, which outlines the steps for creating, publishing, and promoting material that increases brand loyalty and trust.

**Here are two approaches to launching a content marketing strategy:**

**Make newsletters:** Marketing emails, such as newsletters, can drive traffic by providing relevant and intriguing material that encourages readers to click. Wix can help you create your own successful email marketing campaign by providing fully adjustable layouts, marketing automation tools, easy-to-read analytics tracking, and other features.

**Start a blog:** There are numerous reasons why blogging is well worth the time and effort. Aside from the ability to monetize a website, having a blog can increase visitors to your site. Covering a wide range of topics will attract more readers, and thus more users, to your product or service. Blog posts can be repurposed and shared on social media.

Content-wise, having your own blog allows you to communicate your thoughts and ideas in a more personal tone while still exhibiting your level of skill in your industry.

Social networking is another effective approach to reach a larger audience. When you update your website, you can share the news via your social media platforms. However, don't simply market your website. Engage with your audience in a genuine manner.

- **Maintain your professional website:** As your professional website's traffic and visitors increase, you'll need it to perform smoothly. Website maintenance can feel like a daunting task, but it doesn't have to be. There are some simple measures you can take to maintain your website with little expenditure. These include updating your content, such as the contact form, responding to customer feedback, monitoring online inventory and eliminating faulty links, and updating your privacy policy. Maintaining keeps your audience engaged and your website looking professional.

  It's also necessary to check for updates to your software and add-ons at least once a month. Even if your website is well-protected, outdated software can pose a security concern.

**Tip: Looking for a catchy title for your website's domain or subdomain? Use a website name generator to get inspiration and ideas.**

When it comes to developing a professional website, you'll want to employ a website builder, whether DIY or headless, that includes advanced website infrastructure. This includes automatic web hosting, the ability to select and connect a domain name, and security with 24/7 monitoring.

## The importance of social media.

- Direct contact with the target audience:

Thanks to social media networks, you no longer have to phone or email people at random to see whether they are interested in your brand. With practically everyone on social media, your target audience could be just a click away. Using hashtags, you may instantly land your brand on the pages of your target demographic, giving you significant reach.

- Increasing Popularity and Ease:

The capacity to gain popularity is especially important for those in the content and digital marketing fields. Social media platforms provide exactly what this group of people is searching for: more exposure. Carrying out simple, fascinating chores such as answering questions, publishing timings, and so on will ensure that you blow up on these platforms over time. Even while it takes some time, the large profits make it worthwhile in the end.

- Better traffic:

Because there is a wide range of active users on social media, the opportunity for different visitors is increased. Optimizing social media for your specific needs helps ensure that you receive visits and traffic from a variety of people. People are more likely to stumble across your brand or company now that they spend the majority of their time on their phones. Proper use of keywords and other SEO recommendations would also result in increased and improved traffic.

- Create a lasting image:

If you want to ensure that your piece of content makes an imprint on the viewer's brain, social media is the greatest approach to do so. Granted, people do check their emails. But how often do we see people spending hours going through their emails? In contrast, individuals like spending countless hours on their phones scrolling through social media. As a result, if you can successfully optimize your work there, you are sure to leave an impression.

- Collaborations:

Another effective method social media platforms aid businesses is by allowing them to collaborate with suitable accounts. Today, there are numerous influencers on every social media site, each eager to promote the product they believe is most suited to their audience. Businesses wishing to expand typically contact influencers who run paid advertisements on their pages, resulting in high traffic to the company account.

- Availability of Analysis Tools:

Another component of social media that contributes to its popularity among businesses and content creators is the ability to look into insights. As a result, business and content accounts can examine their posts to determine which ones were most popular and why, as well as how to optimize their feed. On Instagram, there is a post insights feature for professional accounts, which allows you to view which posts received the most saves, likes, or reaches.

Get inspired.

Because most content and company pages are public, one may rapidly scroll through their feeds for inspiration. If your account is not performing well in comparison to the other accounts in the field, you can examine their feeds to discover what you're losing out on. Fixing these issues may significantly increase your popularity.

## Success Stories: Building an Online Brand.

### 6 successful brands with unusual beginnings

### AMAZON

**Amazon:** From Online Bookstore to E-Commerce Behemoth.

In 1994, Jeff Bezos started Cadabra, an online bookstore that subsequently became Amazon, one of the world's most successful brands. Initially centered on book sales, Amazon gradually expanded its product offerings to include electronics, apparel, and household items.

Amazon Web Services, Amazon Prime, and Amazon Studios were all created as a result of the brand's ongoing innovation efforts. Today, Amazon dominates the e-commerce landscape, demonstrating the power of pivoting and accepting new opportunities.

**Cadabra was a strange brand name**

Amazon was formerly known as Cadabra, a name taken from the magical word "abracadabra." However, the name Cadabra proved troublesome, as it was frequently mispronounced as "cadaver."

Recognizing the importance of a more appealing and distinctive corporate identity, Bezos chose to redesign the company. Inspired by the size and diversity of the Amazon River, he chose the name "Amazon" to represent the company's ability to provide a wide range of products and services.

Amazon's success was largely due to its early adoption of digital technology.

Amazon's dedication to breaking new ground in technology and customer experience has helped it become one of the most successful brands.

Amazon's proprietary one-click ordering technology, debuted in 1999, substantially shortened the shopping procedure.

Bezos understood early on the importance of diversifying the company's offerings in order to remain competitive. As a result, they launched Amazon Marketplace in 2000, with new items added each.

Amazon Web Services (AWS) was launched in 2006. AWS, a cloud computing platform, has since emerged as a dominating player in the sector, offering cost-effective solutions to startups, companies, and governments alike.

In 2007, Amazon introduced the Kindle, an e-reader that changed the way people read books. The business expanded its entertainment offerings by launching Amazon Prime, which today has millions of customers who enjoy streaming music, movies, and TV shows, as well as free delivery and other perks.

Amazon has seen incredibly stable sales growth.

Interestingly, Amazon has had amazing compounding growth from its inception. For example, sales surpassed $1 billion in just four years. Furthermore, they topped $10 billion in the tenth year and $100 billion in the twentieth year. Currently, their revenue for 2022 surpasses $500 billion. Nonetheless, due to increased competition from Walmart and other stores entering e-commerce, Amazon's growth rate fell to 9% in 2022.

Assume Amazon had preserved the name Cadabra. Will it still be one of the world's most successful brands? Given its experience, my response is a loud YES.

## STARBUCKS

**Starbucks:** From selling ground coffee to a global coffeehouse chain.

Starbucks' development from a modest store selling ground coffee to a global coffeehouse chain is an inspiring story of entrepreneurship, vision, and perseverance. Jerry Baldwin, Zev Siegl, and Gordon Bowker founded Starbucks in 1971, and the first location opened in Seattle's Pike Place Market. Initially, the trio concentrated on selling premium coffee beans, tea, and spices. Howard Schultz joined Starbucks.

It wasn't until 1982, when Howard Schultz joined Starbucks as director of retail operations and marketing, that the concept of a European-style coffeehouse emerged.

Schultz, inspired by the colorful coffee culture he encountered during a business trip to Italy, saw the opportunity to transform Starbucks into a place where people could mingle while drinking coffee. Despite initial opposition from the founders, Schultz's ambition finally prevailed, prompting him to acquire Starbucks in 1987. Starbucks rose to become one of the world's most successful companies during Schultz's leadership.

Starbucks experienced a difficulty in 2008.

In 2008, Starbucks' customer service had deteriorated to the point where their most loyal customers were fleeing. Without a doubt, the brand was on the verge of failure, with a falling stock price, store closures, and massive layoffs.

Starbucks had grown beyond its means in the past five years, expanding into the recording and film industries. Importantly, read our Starbucks case study to see how the collapse prompted a refocus on coffee. Above all, we will demonstrate how Starbucks transformed their customer experience into what we see today.

We also have a piece about how Starbucks has followed Apple's lead by opening numerous gorgeous Starbucks outlets.

## NOKIA

**Nokia:** From Pulp Mill to Telecommunications Titan.

Nokia's humble roots date back to 1865, when it was established as a pulp factory in Finland. Over the years, the corporation expanded into a variety of industries, including rubber, cables, and electronics.

Nokia entered the telecommunications business in the 1980s and grew to become the world's leading mobile phone manufacturer by the late 1990s. At the time, Nokia was regarded one of the most successful brands.

Despite being threatened by the rise of smartphones, Nokia shifted its focus to telecoms infrastructure and licensed its brand for new devices, demonstrating the value of adaptability.

And now, in the 2020s, Nokia needs a fresh pivot.

# 3M

The famous trivial chase question is, "What does 3M stand for?"

Minnesota Mining and Manufacturing Company, today known as 3M, was created in 1902 to mine corundum, a mineral used in grinding wheels.

However, the entrepreneurs quickly discovered that the material they were mining was of inferior quality. Rather than giving up, 3M shifted its attention to inventing new products.

Today, 3M is known for a diverse range of products, including adhesive tapes, protective films, medical supplies, and electronic devices, demonstrating that failure may pave the road to becoming one of the most successful brands.

Wrigley: From Soap and Baking Powder to Chewing Gum Empire.

Wrigley, the well-known chewing gum company, was founded in 1891 as a soap and baking powder manufacturer.

To encourage clients, founder William Wrigley Jr. offered complimentary chewing gum with every purchase of his products. The gum quickly became more popular than the soap and baking powder, prompting Wrigley to concentrate completely on creating and selling chewing gum. Wrigley's unique marketing methods and devotion to quality contributed to its status as one of the most successful brands.

## AVON

**Avon:** From Door-to-Door Book Sales to the Beauty Giant

David H. McConnell established Avon in 1886 as the California Perfume Company. McConnell initially sold books door-to-door, but sought to entice female consumers by offering little perfume samples. He quickly learned that perfume was more popular than books, so he shifted his concentration to beauty products.

Today, Avon is one of the world's most successful companies and the leading direct marketer of cosmetics and personal care items. This is an excellent example of how a side dish can become the primary attraction.

# CHAPTER 3:

# OVERCOMING COMMON CHALLENGES - ADDRESSING SELF-DOUBT

**How to overcome self-doubt.**
**What is self-doubt exactly?** Self-doubt begins with a lack of confidence in oneself or one's talents.

Self-doubt, in its more complicated form, can be defined as uncertainty regarding the veracity of any situation.

Self-doubt in various forms is extremely prevalent, and most of us will experience it at some point or another. However, having this perspective can prevent you from reaching your goals.

If you're constantly tormented by self-doubt, it's a good idea to step back and assess the detrimental influence it's having on your life or job.

From there, you can focus on implementing self-confidence boosting tactics to assist you increase your self-esteem.

- **Reflect on Opportunities:** Self-doubt frequently causes us to rationalize a circumstance based on our emotional state. We may be terrified of failing, looking terrible, or taking on more than we believe we can handle. Our brain can easily create excuses and self-justifications for not taking advantage of opportunities.

    Consider the opportunities you turned away. What reasons did you offer yourself? Were they valid causes or simply excuses? Excuses are mental obstacles that we create to keep ourselves back.

- **Follow Good Energy:** According to a popular adage, "We are the average of the five people we spend the most time with." The people we spend time with can have a significant impact on us, even if we are unaware of it. Brain plasticity research has shown that experiences can rearrange neuronal networks in the brain.

Who is the person you spend the most time with? How do they affect you? Do you feel better or worse about yourself after spending time with them?

- **Increasing your self-awareness:** Self-awareness might be one of the most effective personal growth strategies. Make use of it by identifying the underlying causes of your self-doubt. What scenarios cause you to have doubts about yourself? If you lack skill in a certain area, make a commitment to improving it.

  **For example,** it could be a phobia of giving presentations or making cold calls. Almost anything can be learned. Go acquire the training you need, or hire a coach to help you.

- **Practice self-compassion:** While it may feel natural to provide compassion to others, it can be difficult to balance self-criticism with self-compassion. Self-compassion is simply being kind to oneself. According to studies, there is a substantial link between self-compassion and better mental health, including less anxiety, increased life satisfaction, and higher self-esteem. Self-compassion can help you build emotional resilience.

- **Think for yourself:** Seeking other people's opinions and suggestions can be beneficial. However, if you constantly ask people for their opinions before making judgments, you may be undermining your own confidence.

  **For example,** if you're working on a presentation, creating a website, or starting a new project and keep changing it depending on criticism, you risk losing your voice and the ultimate result being a diluted version of your vision.

  Consider some advice, but also make the decision that seems right for you.

- Trust Your Values In today's fast-paced, ever-changing surroundings, individuals who can navigate complexity can achieve amazing results.

  The characteristic that drives the majority of entrepreneurs is "trusting your gut and values." We are increasingly being asked to make hasty decisions based on limited information. When you know what you stand for and what is important to you, it is simpler to make decisions that are consistent with your values. Self-doubt can impair our capacity to make vital decisions, but knowing yourself and living your principles is one of the most effective remedies.

- **Start Shipping:** Seth Godin, an American entrepreneur and author, frequently encourages people to "start shipping!" If you're an artist who is hesitant to exhibit your work because you don't believe it's your finest yet, it's sometimes better to attempt than not try at all.

  Self-doubt can cause mental paralysis. Having the courage to start can go a long way.

**The Takeaway**

Many people have self-doubt. Finding solutions to overcome it might boost your happiness and motivation to attempt new things.

## Managing Your Time Effectively

Finding the optimal time management approach for you is determined by your personality, self-motivation, and amount of self-discipline. You can improve your time management by applying some or all of the ten tactics listed below.

- ☐ **Know how you spend your time:** A time journal is an effective approach to track how you spend your time. For a week or two, keep track of your activities in 15-minute intervals. Evaluate the outcomes.
  - Did you finish what you needed to do?
  - Which chores take the most time?
  - What time of day are you most productive?
  - Where do you spend the most of your time (work, family, personal, or recreation)?

Identifying your most time-consuming duties and determining whether you are allocating your time to the most important activities will help you decide on a course of action. Knowing how long ordinary things take can help you plan and estimate how much time you have available for other activities. There are numerous apps available to assist you keep track of your time, as discussed in Strategy 3.

- ☐ **Set Priorities**: To properly manage your time, you must distinguish between what is important and what is urgent (MacKenzie 1990). Experts agree that the most important jobs are rarely the most urgent. However, we tend to let urgent responsibilities take over our life. Covey, Merrill, and Merrill (1994) divide activities into four quadrants in their Time Management Matrix: urgent, not urgent, important, and not important. While urgent and important activities must be completed, Covey et al. recommend devoting less time to non-important activities (regardless of urgency) in order to free up time for non-urgent but significant activities. Focusing on these vital activities gives you more control over your time and may limit the amount of critical chores that become urgent.

|  | **Urgent** | **Not Urgent** |
|---|---|---|
| Important | <ul><li>Please complete these chores as soon as possible.</li><li>Examples:</li><li>Submit your job application by 5 p.m.</li><li>Pick up the ill child from school.</li><li>Call a plumber to fix the leaky toilet.</li></ul> | <ul><li>Defer these duties until all urgent and critical activities are done.</li><li>Examples:</li><li>Schedule a dentist appointment.</li><li>Respond to a coworker's email</li></ul> |

|  |  | on an upcoming event.<br>• Plan a family reunion. |
|---|---|---|
| Not Important | • Delegate these responsibilities to the proper persons who can handle them.<br>• Examples:<br>• Help your son with his schoolwork. | • Delete these tasks; they are often time wasters.<br>• Examples:<br>• Respond to the social media |

|  | - Pull weeds from flower beds.<br>- Make dinner for the family. | - remarks.<br>- Online shopping.<br>- Finish watching the TV program. |

Creating a "to do" list is a simple technique to prioritize. Whether you need a daily, weekly, or monthly list is determined by your lifestyle. Keep your list-making under control. Instead of setting goals or creating multi-step plans, list doable activities. Organize your "to do" list in order of priority (important and urgent). You can categorize objects as high priority, medium priority, or low priority; number them in order of priority; or utilize a color-coding scheme. The idea is to mark off the highest priority items rather than the most items (MacKenzie, 1990). A prioritized "to do" list allows you to set boundaries and say "no" to things that may be intriguing or create a sense of accomplishment but do not align with your core priorities.

☐ **Use a planning tool:** Experts in time management propose utilizing a customized planning tool to boost productivity. Personal planning resources include planners, calendars, phone apps, wall charts, index cards, pocket diaries, and notebooks. Writing down your tasks, schedules, and things to remember allows your mind to focus on your priorities. Auditory learners might prefer to dictate their thoughts instead. The goal is to pick one planning tool that works for you and utilize it regularly.

**When use a planning tool:**

Always keep your information on the gadget itself. Taking notes elsewhere and having to transfer them afterward is inefficient and loses time.

Review your planning tool on a daily basis.

Maintain a list of your priorities in your planning tool and refer to it regularly.

Maintain synchronization among planning tools. If you keep more than one, make sure your phone, computer, and paper planners all match.

Maintain a backup system.

Apps on your phone might be useful planning tools. Apps are often divided into one of the following categories:

Time Trackers: Become conscious of how you spend your time.

Time Savers: Boost productivity and eliminate time-wasting habits.

Task managers prioritize and organize work to better time management.

Habit Developers: Develop good habits to promote time management.

4. Get organized.

Disorganization causes poor time management. According to research, clutter has a significant detrimental impact on perceived well-being (Roster, 2016). Get organized to help you manage your time better.

Create three boxes (or corners of a room) labeled "Keep," "Give Away," and "Toss." Sort the objects into these boxes. Discard objects from your

"Toss" box. Your "Give Away" box may contain goods you wish to sell, donate, or toss.

The following step is to shorten the time you spend processing information. For example, chores like email might consume your entire day. To avoid wasting time, develop an email organizing system that allows you to handle the content in each email as quickly as possible. Keep track of what's where via folders, flagging, or a color-coded system.

- ☐ **Schedule appropriately:** Scheduling is more than merely documenting what needs to be done (such as meetings and appointments). Make sure to schedule time for the things you wish to do. To schedule well, you must first understand yourself. Your time log should assist you determine when you are most productive and aware. Schedule your most difficult tasks for when you have the most energy. Set aside time for your highest-priority activities first, and keep it free of interruptions.

Schedule little tasks like writing an email, making a grocery list, reading, watching webinars, or listening to podcasts during long rides or while waiting for a call or appointment. Make the most of time that would otherwise be lost. Avoid engaging in nonproductive activities such as gaming or scrolling through social media. Set aside around three-fourths of your day for creative tasks such as planning, brainstorming, and thinking.

- ☐ **Delegate: Get Help from Others:** Delegating involves giving someone else responsibility for a task, allowing you to devote more time to things that require your skill. Identify jobs that others can do and assign them to the right person(s). Select someone who has the necessary abilities, expertise, interest, and authority to complete the assignment. Be specific. Define the work and your expectations while giving the person the opportunity to personalize it. Check in on the person's progress on a regular basis and offer any aid you can, but avoid taking on too much responsibility. Finally, commend the individual for a job well done or provide ideas for improvement if necessary. (Dowd and Sundheim, 2005). Another option to acquire assistance is to "buy" time by purchasing things or services that save time. For example, hiring someone to mow your lawn or clean your house, or participating in a carpool for your children's extracurricular activities, frees up time for other pursuits. Hiring someone for specific work can save you time and is often worth the expense.

☐ **Stop procrastinating:** People postpone tasks for a variety of reasons. Perhaps the task appears daunting or unpleasant. To help you quit procrastinating, consider "eating the big frog first." A statement often attributed to Mark Twain once said, "If it's your job to eat a frog today, do it first thing in the morning." And if it's your job to devour two frogs, eat the bigger one first." Procrastinating on unpleasant chores is known as "big frogs." Complete these tasks as your first step of the day to get them out of the way. Another alternative is to "snowball" your projects by dividing them down into smaller chunks, doing preliminary activities, and then finishing the bigger task at hand. Whether you choose the "big frog first" or "snowball" technique, include a reward system for accomplished tasks to help you stay motivated.

- ☐ **Manage Time Wasters**

Implement these basic methods to reduce or eliminate the amount of time spent on these tasks.

Handheld devices.

Use voice-to-text services like transcribed voicemails to make notes or compose emails and text messages while on the road.

Avoid small conversation. Stay focused.

Take any essential action right after a call.

Set screen time limitations and assess your digital wellness on a regular basis (see to Strategy 10).

Plan breaks from your devices.

Set aside time to check and respond to emails, but avoid accumulating too many to sort.

Turn off email notifications.

Handle each object only once, if possible.

Immediately delete or unsubscribe from spam emails.

Keep your address books up to date and organized.

Use the built-in shortcuts to sort email.

Unexpected Visitors.

Make time for face-to-face visits.

Inform people about your time limits and gently offer to reschedule.

Determine a mutually acceptable time limit for the visit.

When someone arrives at the door, stand up and hold your meeting standing to keep it brief.

In-Person and Virtual Meetings

Understand the purpose of the meeting in advance.

Arrive early.

Start and terminate meetings on time.

Create an agenda and stick to it. Use a timed agenda if necessary.

Don't plan meetings unless they're really necessary and have a clear purpose or agenda.

Use recording software or assign a note-taker.

Family Obligations

Use and sync virtual calendars to facilitate communication among busy family members.

Make each family member responsible for checking the master calendar for any potential conflicts.

Create a centralized location or agreed-upon app for publishing communications like appointment reminders, announcements, and messages.

- ☐ **Avoid multitasking:** Psychological research has demonstrated that multitasking does not save time. In reality, the opposite is frequently true. Switching from one activity to another takes time and reduces production (Rubinstein, Meyer, and Evans, 2001). Routine multitasking may cause trouble concentrating and keeping focus. Do your best to focus on one activity at a time by keeping your workspace distraction-free, including turning off notifications on your gadgets, and scheduling dedicated time for specific projects.
- ☐ **Stay healthy:** Self-care and attentiveness are valuable investments of time. Setting aside time to relax or do nothing helps you

refresh physically and mentally, allowing you to complete activities more quickly and effortlessly. Monitor your screen time as part of your digital well-being, and set boundaries to stay healthy. According to a Google study, four out of five study participants who made actions to improve their digital well-being say their overall well-being has improved (Google, 2019). Setting time restrictions or using built-in software on electronic devices such as phones and tablets can help you maintain your digital wellbeing. Blue light blockers and grayscale mode may also benefit your digital well-being. Set a time each night to turn off all digital gadgets to allow your mind to relax; this can also help with your sleep schedule.

Unfortunately, poor time management and excessive screen time can lead to weariness, mood swings, and more frequent illness. To alleviate stress, reward yourself for successful time management. Before proceeding to the next action, take a moment to acknowledge that you have completed a large task or obstacle.

# Personal Story: Overcoming Obstacles

Inspirational Stories: Famous People Overcoming Failure and Struggle

Another guest, **Leonard Kim**, was practically destitute. He couldn't afford to pay his rent or

eat lunch, so he moved in with his grandparents. He recognized he needed to do something with his life and chose to blog. He currently has over ten million viewers and operates a very successful business.

**Paul Isenberg** discovered his wife Nicole had Stage IV Hodgkin's lymphoma cancer while she was nine months pregnant with their child. She underwent six and a half years of treatment before passing. His experience showed him the value of having the right support to get through a difficult period. It inspired him to form an organization to help others by raising funds for expenses not covered by insurance, such as driving to treatments, lodging, and other costs that can total more than $30,000 per year. He now helps families afford such fees through his company, Bringing Hope Home.

**Cheryl Hunter** set out to become a model. She flew to Europe for the first time, and, just as in films like Taken, she was kidnapped, raped, and left for dead. She now devotes her time to helping others see that there is hope. Her story was told in an excellent TED presentation, and she now spends her time teaching people how to be successful, self-confident, and joyful no matter what challenges they face.

When we look at images of these folks, we cannot perceive their problems. Sometimes it appears that folks have numerous advantages.

If you have a voice in your head telling you that you can't do anything, you probably can't. If you listen to that voice, I believe you can. I spend a lot of time working with people to increase their curiosity.

# There are four factors that can keep you from being interested, and I believe they will keep you from succeeding.

These four things are **fear**, **preconceptions**, **technology**, and the **environment**. If you can recognize your fears, change the voice in your head that makes incorrect assumptions, embrace technology, and recognize how your life experiences have influenced your decisions, I believe you can truly embrace curiosity, which will lead to motivation and, ultimately, success. The actual trick is that you must begin today. Every day you put off working toward your next objective is a day squandered.

# CHAPTER 4:

# MARKET YOUR SKILLS

## Effective Social Media Strategies.

- **Understand your target audience.**

Knowing who you want your message to reach is the core of every successful social media campaign. Once you've determined who you want to market to, you can concentrate on developing high-quality content that will resonate with them and endure over time. Remember that trends come and go, but quality content that adheres to your brand's values will always be most effective. Nowadays, everyone wants a tailored social media experience, so understanding your target audience's preferences increases their likelihood of engaging with your post and eventually converting to loyal consumers.

BRIDGE knows actual individuals and owns their data. This means we gather vital information on each member of our audience. With this information, we can put together a group of people who are exactly aligned with your brand's offering and aspirations. And because we already know their online habits, we can tell you which platforms they are most active on, so you don't have to worry about wasting ad dollars. If your concentration is on eco-friendly items, for example, we'll find people who care about sustainability and establish a targeted audience. BRIDGE helps you connect with an audience who actually resonates with your business, making your social media activities more effective.

- **Select The Right Platforms.**

There are numerous platforms available, making it difficult to determine which ones will best serve your advertising objectives. The average person has eight separate profiles on various social media platforms. distinct social media platforms tend to serve distinct goals. For example, if someone is looking for graphics and creative inspiration, they will most likely visit Instagram or Pinterest. LinkedIn is the finest site to find professional development tools and career assistance. Knowing what purpose your firm serves and where your target audience is most engaged will help you choose which platform is appropriate for delivering your adverts.

Because BRIDGE is all about people-based knowledge, we truly understand our audience. And because we already know their online activities, we can tell you which platforms they are most active on, saving you time guessing. We'll identify your target demographic and select the platforms that best meet your objectives. In digital marketing, choosing the proper social platforms is like striking the bullseye, so let us assist you make an informed decision.

- **Draw Them In With Content**.

Once you've identified your target audience and the best platforms for reaching them, content becomes your next secret weapon. Creating compelling content is more than just attracting people's attention; it's also about keeping them engaged. Assume you're speaking directly with your customer. Your material should feel like it was created specifically for them.

Quality and involvement are your allies. High-quality pictures and interesting stories will bring people in, keep them intrigued, and frequently inspire them to submit their own ideas. Next, consistency in your brand's voice and imagery is essential. When your audience identifies your style, trust and loyalty will increase. Sticking to a consistent tone, whether casual or professional, helps to create a sense of familiarity.

Stay current with unique occasions and trends. Holidays and festivals are ideal opportunities to interact with your audience on a personal level. And remember, BRIDGE has your back. We have a thorough grasp of your target demographic, and our specialized creative team will assist you in creating content that truly resonates. When your content sparkles, your audience will remain and spread the word. So make your content a star and watch your social media presence skyrocket!

- **Keep Them Engaged.**

Engaging with your target audience on your company's social media sites is the key to effective digital marketing. Once you've captured their interest with your adverts, you should urge them to interact with your organic postings as well. It's all about making genuine connections with the people who actually support your business. Think of social media as a virtual gathering of friends. Responding to comments is like having a conversation. Responding to a praise or a question demonstrates that you are listening and value their opinions.

But don't simply leave comments; start conversations too! Ask questions, conduct surveys, or do anything else that will get people talking. This allows you to better understand them and makes them feel important. If there is a concern or problem, express it freely and gently. Turning a bad into a positive demonstrates that you want to make things right.

Remember that these are actual people behind the screen. Engaging is more than just selling products; it's about making connections. When you connect, you are not just earning customers, but also developing brand champions.

Analyze and adapt to new strategies.

Once your ads have gone live, campaign analysis will allow you to see the results of your efforts. At this stage, you will have the ability to fine-tune your efforts and improve your targeting over time.

First and foremost, you want to feel as if you're communicating with real individuals rather than shouting into the vacuum. Our visual campaign data shows you exactly who is engaged with your brand, visiting your store, and becoming a client.

Second, data analysis allows you to finetune your strategy. It displays what is on target and what isn't. It's like having intimate knowledge of what your audience likes and hates.

Finally, it shows you who in your audience is close to making a purchase but not quite there yet. Not everyone acts right away, and that's okay. With our data, you may retarget customers who expressed interest but require a push.

Remember that data can help you make more educated judgments. Data analysis and open campaign reporting allow you to make informed, successful decisions for your social media strategy rather than shooting in the dark.

## Using Email Marketing To Engage Customers

Email marketing has been around for decades, but it remains one of the most successful ways to reach out and interact with clients. In fact, according to a recent research, 81% of small businesses use email marketing as their major customer acquisition method, and it's easy to see why. With the correct strategy, email marketing may help you connect with your customers on a more personal level, establish brand loyalty, and ultimately increase sales. So, if you want to improve consumer engagement and boost your bottom line, understand how to use email marketing efficiently. In this post, we'll go over everything you need to know to launch a successful email marketing campaign, from developing your email list to drafting the ideal subject line, and everything in between. So, whether you're an experienced email marketer or just getting started, keep reading to learn how to use email marketing to increase consumer engagement.

- **Create a high-quality email list.**

"Building a high-quality email list" refers to the process of gathering a group of people who have willingly volunteered their contact information with you, such as their email addresses, so that you can send marketing messages. The idea is to build a list of people who are truly interested in your company, products, or services and are more likely to respond to your email content. To accomplish this, you must employ ethical and transparent strategies to acquire subscribers who opt in to receive your emails. This includes avoiding questionable methods such as purchasing email lists, spamming, or offering deceptive incentives to entice individuals to join up.

Instead, you can employ a variety of strategies, like delivering quality material, offering unique deals or discounts, organizing webinars, and running contests. Remember that developing a high-quality email list takes time and work, but it's worthwhile since it allows you to interact with people who are really interested in what you have to offer, resulting in increased customer engagement and sales.

- **Developing an Effective Email Marketing Strategy**

"Creating an effective email marketing strategy" entails devising a strategy for using email marketing to reach out to your target audience and engage with them in a way that supports your business objectives. To develop an effective strategy, you must first define your target audience, identify your business goals, and decide how email marketing might help you reach them. You should also consider the types of email content you want to publish, such as newsletters, promotional emails, or event invitations, as well as how often you want to send them. Timing, tone, and personalization are all crucial aspects to consider when creating emails that appeal with your subscribers and urge them to take action.

Furthermore, you should create a system for monitoring the performance of your email marketing efforts, such as tracking open rates, click-through rates, and conversion rates, so that you can make data-driven decisions about how to enhance your strategy in the future. Developing an effective email marketing plan requires time and work, but when done correctly, it can be a powerful tool for engaging with your audience, building brand loyalty, and driving more revenue.

- **Writing effective subject lines and preheader text**

"Writing compelling subject lines and preheader text" is a critical component of developing great email marketing campaigns that capture your audience's attention and motivate them to open your messages. The subject line is the first thing your subscribers see when your email arrives in their inbox, so it should be catchy, succinct, and related to the content of your email. A well-written subject line might stimulate the recipient's interest, instill urgency, or offer a clear value that drives them to open the email.

In addition, the preheader text is a small line of text that shows adjacent to the subject line in most email programs. This phrase previews the content of your email and is an opportunity to convince your readers to open it. You should attempt to make your preheader material useful, entertaining, and relevant to your subject line.

When crafting subject lines and preheader material, keep your audience in mind and think about what they will find most appealing. Personalization, comedy, urgency, and other strategies can be used to generate a sense of relevance and engagement. However, it is also critical to avoid misleading or clickbait subject lines, which can undermine your brand's reputation or result in lower engagement rates. You may raise open rates and the overall efficacy of your email marketing efforts by generating captivating subject lines and preheader text that are relevant to the content of your email.

- **Creating engaging email content that resonates with your readers.**

To create engaging email content that speaks to your subscribers' needs and interests and encourages them to take action, you must first understand your audience and tailor your messaging to their preferences. Factors such as demographics, interests, and paid.

When creating content, aim to provide value to your subscribers by providing relevant and useful information, such as tips, how-to guides, or exclusive offers. You can also use visual elements like images, videos, or infographics to make your content more engaging and easier to consume. Additionally, you should keep your messaging concise, scannable, and easy to read, and use a clear call-to-action to encourage subscribers to take the next step, such as

It's important to remember that your email content should reflect your brand's voice and values, while also being respectful and empathetic to your subscriber's needs. You should also test different types of content and messaging to see what resonates best with your audience, and use data and feedback to continuously improve your approach. By crafting engaging email content that speaks to your subscriber's needs and interests, you can improve customer engagement, but

Using segmentation and customisation to increase engagement

"Using segmentation and personalization to improve engagement" is a powerful way to tailor your email marketing campaigns to your audience's preferences and needs. Segmentation involves dividing your email list into smaller groups based on shared characteristics, such as age, location, purchase history, or interests, while personalization involves creating content and messaging that speaks directly to each subscriber.

By segmenting your email list and using personalization, you can deliver more relevant

83

and targeted messages to your subscribers, which can help increase engagement and drive conversions. For example, you can send personalized product recommendations based on a subscriber's purchase history or location, or you can use their first name in the subject line or greeting to create a more personal connection.

When using segmentation and personalization, it's important to ensure that your data is accurate and up-to-date, and that your messaging is respectful and non-intrusive. You should also test different segmentation and personalization strategies to see what resonates best with your audience, and use data and feedback to continuously improve your strategy.

Overall, segmentation and personalization may help you design more focused, relevant, and engaging email messages that speak directly to your audience's needs and interests, resulting in higher engagement and better commercial results.

- **Creating mobile-friendly emails that look beautiful on all devices.**

"Designing mobile-friendly emails that look great on any device" is critical to the success of your email marketing campaigns in today's mobile-first world. As more and more people access their emails on mobile devices, it's important to design emails that are optimized for smaller screens and can be easily read and navigated on any device.

To create mobile-friendly emails, you should use a responsive design that adjusts the layout and formatting of your email to fit the size of the screen it's being viewed on. This means using a single-column layout, larger fonts, and clear, easy-to-tap buttons and links. You should also optimize your images for mobile devices, ensuring they're sized appropriately and load quickly.

In addition, you should test your emails on various devices and email clients to ensure that they look and work properly. You can utilize email marketing software with mobile preview features to check how your emails will appear on different devices.

When writing mobile-friendly emails, keep your messaging simple and scannable, as mobile consumers have shorter attention spans. You can use subheadings, bullet points, and other formatting features to make your material consumable.

Designing mobile-friendly emails that look fantastic on any device can improve your subscribers' user experience and increase engagement with your email campaigns, leading to better results and more successful email marketing for your organization.

- **Optimizing email send times for optimum impact.**

"Optimizing email send times for maximum impact" entails establishing the optimum time to send your emails in order to improve engagement and response rates. Sending emails at the proper time increases the likelihood that your subscribers will open, read, and act on them.

To optimize email send times, you should first understand your audience's habits and preferences, which include factors such as their time zone, work schedule, and when they are most likely to check their email. You can gather this information using data from your email marketing software or by conducting surveys.

Once you have a good understanding of your audience's habits and preferences, you can begin testing different send times to see what works best. You can send emails at different times and on different days, and track metrics such as open rates, click-through rates, and conversions to determine which times are most successful.

It's crucial to remember that the best send time may differ depending on your audience and the purpose of your email. For instance, a promotional email may perform better when sent on a weekday morning, whereas a newsletter or instructional email may work better when sent on the weekend.

By optimizing your email send times, you may boost engagement and response rates, resulting in better outcomes for your email marketing efforts.

A/B testing to increase open and click-through rates.

"A/B testing to improve open and click-through rates" is a powerful technique that involves sending two different versions of an email to a small portion of your audience, and then measuring which version performs better based on metrics like open rates, click-through rates, and conversions.

A/B testing can assist you in making data-driven decisions about your email marketing campaigns by providing insights into what messaging, design, and calls-to-action are most effective for your audience. For instance, you can test different subject lines, email templates, images, and copy to see what resonates best with your subscribers.

To conduct an A/B test, you should first identify the element you want to test and create two versions of your email that differ only in that element. Then, randomly assign a small portion of your audience to each group and send the emails. After a predetermined period of time, you can analyze the results to see which version performed better.

To ensure the reliability and accuracy of your A/B test findings, only test one variable at a time and utilize statistically significant sample sizes.

Using A/B testing to boost open and click-through rates may optimize your email marketing efforts and increase engagement with your audience. Over time, you can use the data and insights from A/B testing to continuously refine your approach and produce more effective email campaigns.

- **Assessing and assessing email marketing performance**

"Measuring and analyzing email marketing performance" is an essential component of any effective email marketing plan. By tracking important metrics and analyzing your email campaign data, you may acquire insights into what works well, what doesn't, and how you can improve future efforts.

Open rates, click-through rates, conversion rates, and unsubscribe rates are some of the key metrics you should track when measuring email marketing performance, as they can help you understand how your subscribers interact with your emails and whether your campaigns are meeting your objectives.

To measure and analyze email marketing performance, you should use an email marketing software that provides detailed analytics and reporting. Many email marketing tools provide dashboards that make it easy to track and analyze your campaign data, as well as insights into your audience's behavior and preferences.

When analyzing your email marketing performance, it's important to look not only at individual metrics, but also at how they relate to each other and to your overall business goals. For example, if your click-through rates are high but your conversion rates are low, you may need to improve your call-to-action or landing page design.

Regularly measuring and analyzing your email marketing performance allows you to identify areas for improvement, make data-driven decisions, and continuously optimize your email campaigns for better results. This can help you build stronger relationships with your audience, drive more traffic and sales, and ultimately achieve your business goals.

Using automation to optimize your email marketing efforts

Email marketing automation is a powerful way to save time, increase efficiency, and deliver more personalized and relevant emails to your subscribers. This involves using software to send triggered emails based on specific actions or behaviors, such as subscribing to your list, abandoning a cart, or making a purchase.

By automating your email marketing efforts, you can free up time to focus on other important tasks while also sending timely and relevant messages to your subscribers. For example, you can set up a welcome email series that automatically sends a series of onboarding messages to new subscribers, or a cart abandonment email that sends a reminder to shoppers who left items in their cart but did not complete their purchase.

Email marketing automation can help you segment your audience more effectively by automatically assigning subscribers to specific segments based on their behaviors or interests, allowing you to deliver more personalized and relevant emails that are more likely to engage subscribers and drive conversions.

To use automation in your email marketing efforts, you should first identify which workflows and triggers you want to automate. Then, you can use email marketing software with automation features to set up your workflows and triggers, as well as track and analyze the performance of your automated campaigns.

By using automation to streamline your email marketing efforts, you can save time, increase efficiency, and send more personalized and relevant messages to your subscribers. This can help you build stronger relationships with your audience, increase engagement, and ultimately achieve your email marketing goals.

# Entrepreneur Insights: Successful Marketing Tactics

What You Should Do to Achieve Entrepreneurial Success

Have a strong and clear vision - Every entrepreneurial journey should start with a compelling, actionable vision. Consider the objective of your business and your long-term goals. This information will help drive your decision-making process, inspire your team, and attract stakeholders who share your vision.

Always have a growth mindset. To actually attain entrepreneurial success, you must be constantly thinking about business expansion. Adopt a growth mindset that values invention, creativity, and resilience. If you fail or make a mistake, view it as a learning opportunity. Constantly seek methods to improve and evolve as an entrepreneur. This approach not only helps you deal with unforeseen obstacles, but it also inspires your team to strive for excellence.

- **Conduct Market Research:** Don't underestimate the value of market research, and don't believe you know everything there is to know about your sector. Before you establish or scale your business, conduct extensive market research. Understand your target customer, their problem issues, and what differentiates your services and products.
- **Build a Great Workforce:** Regardless of your sector or business size, you should always strive to create the greatest workforce possible. After all, your team is the foundation for your success. Employ people who compliment your abilities and share your enthusiasm. Encourage teamwork, communication, and constant

learning. You may not realize it, but a great team is critical to overcoming challenges and generating corporate success.
- **Create a Strong Brand Identity:** There are many competitors out there, so you must guarantee that your firm stands out and is remembered. This does not merely entail having a good logo. It entails creating a consistent brand voice, ethos, visuals, and messaging. This helps to establish trust and loyalty among your target audience.
- **Use Marketing to Promote Your Business:** People need to know who you are and what you do, and that's where marketing comes in. Create a comprehensive marketing strategy that includes digital platforms, content marketing, and social media to spread the word. Tailor your approach to your target demographic and adjust your strategy as new digital marketing trends emerge.
- **Don't Rush Into Scaling Your firm:** While it's easy to start scaling your firm anytime you have a burst of success, you should approach scalability carefully. You must

guarantee that your company's infrastructure, operations, and resources can support the growth. Your company must be able to expand while maintaining high-quality products and services.

Thriving in Business is Within Reach.
As you can see, entrepreneurs can achieve success and thrive in business. However, it does not happen without a lot of effort and involvement from you. As a business owner, you must do all possible to incorporate insights and strategies into your operations. You must use feedback and continually change your business to satisfy market demands. Entrepreneurship is not an easy road, but it is rewarding in terms of business success. Before you know it, you'll be doing well in business.

# CHAPTER 5:

# MONETIZING YOUR KNOWLEDGE - EARNING MONEY ONLINE

## 20 Ways to Earn Money from Home

There are numerous ways to work from home, whether you want a full-time job or a side gig to supplement your income. Among its numerous advantages, home-based employment provides a healthy work-life balance and the freedom to set your own schedule. Reviewing options for making money at home will help you decide which ones you want to pursue.

**Here are 20 things you could consider to make money from home:**
- ☐ **Become a Virtual Assistant.**

A virtual assistant (VA) provides administrative services to clients while working remotely, such as from home. They execute a variety of tasks for their clients, including making travel arrangements, conducting web research, and checking emails. They may also go with their clients or work at their offices to complete necessary activities.

☐ **Pet Sitting**

If you enjoy animals, you could pursue pet sitting. It's a good way to make money by watching people's pets at home. However, most sitters work at the pet owner's house.

If you work from home, consider investing in marketing and insurance. In addition, you may want to consult with an accountant, bookkeeper, and lawyer about responsibility.

☐ **Sell your belongings online.**

Examine your home for goods you no longer use, such as furniture, clothing, books, technology, and toys your children have outgrown. You can then post such things on various e-commerce websites to attract buyers. It is critical to capture clear, high-resolution images of your work. Perform online research to determine how much similar things sell for, and then price your items competitively.

☐ **Tutor pupils online.**

Use your skills in specific areas or your SAT/ACT knowledge to provide online tutoring to high school and college students. Promote your services at local schools to find children who require them. You can also apply to work for reputable online tutoring companies.

☐ **Start a blog.**

If you have a specific passion in a topic, you may start a blog and promote it on social media to attract an audience interested in learning more about it. If your blog has a large enough following, you can generate money by posting adverts on it. For example, you may establish a blog that reviews local restaurants or compares different drinks.

☐ **Sell services online**.

There are numerous websites where specialists can offer their expertise on a contract or per-project basis. You could provide services such as graphic or website design, link development, programming, animation, or video creation. Many websites can help you market professional services to local and international customers.

☐ **Create sales funnels.**

Many companies utilize automated sales funnels to market and sell their products and services. Sales funnels are collections of prospective customers at various phases of the sales cycle. Many business owners are ignorant of the benefits of using a sales funnel to expand their organization. Consider creating a business selling sales funnels. You may create them with a variety of low-cost tools.

☐ **Sell consulting services.**

Consulting is another option for making money online while working from home. If you're an expert in a specific industry, you might be able to find people who will pay you to advise them on their company or personal goals. Launching and promoting your own blog is one approach to demonstrate your extensive expertise to others. Another option is to post regular content on professional networking websites.

As a digital marketing expert, you may help business owners grow their social media presence. You can utilize social media to promote your professional information at a minimal or no expense. After acquiring a few clients, you may be able to quickly expand your firm through word-of-mouth marketing. You can meet with clients virtually and set appointments at times that suit your needs.

☐ **Start an internet store.**

While huge e-commerce shops dominate the market, people are also looking for good offers online. Consider creating a sales funnel for yourself to attract visitors and customers to your products and services. For example, you could open an online pet supplies store where you source and curate the best pet products for customers on your website.

☐ **Create webinars.**

Webinars are an excellent approach to sell items or provide advice because they normally follow a standard framework and template that is simple to understand. For example, they may provide visual representations of specific steps and provide simple directions for newcomers. Once you understand how to present excellent webinars, you may begin earning money from home. Webinars allow you to demonstrate to your audience the additional value they would receive if they purchased your product or service.

- ☐ **Manage social media accounts for small enterprises.**

Small businesses frequently require assistance with keeping their social media accounts, and many choose to hire someone for a few hours per week rather than hiring someone to manage social media full-time.

Learn about the various social media channels and choose one or two to concentrate in. Then decide on a certain industry in which you want to work. Finally, contact the several businesses in your neighborhood that you believe you might most effectively assist.

- ☐ **Create online classes.**

If you have a marketable expertise that others would like to learn, you may consider creating your own online course. You can design your course on a variety of sites. Once produced and launched, an online course can provide a significant source of passive revenue.

- ☐ **Sell affiliate marketing offers.**

Affiliate marketing is a straightforward, well-established way to make money from home by selling other companies' products and services, especially if you already have a website, blog, or social media account with a high volume of quality visitors. There are several websites that promote affiliate offers, and you can share a personalized code with your audience to use when making purchases. The code links the purchase to you, and the vendor pays you a set sum for each sale. Take the time to study your audience and what they are most interested in, and then hunt for the best offer for them.

☐ **Launch a podcast.**

A podcast is another excellent way to share your skills with a virtual audience. Finding a specific niche and providing outstanding content to develop your audience are essential for podcast success. Once you've created an audience and are getting a lot of downloads every episode, you can look into ways to monetize your podcast, such as selling adverts and affiliate marketing.

While you may want to conduct some research to understand how to develop, edit, and promote a podcast, if you are an expert on a specific field, it is a worthwhile endeavor.

☐ **Take a babysitting job.**

Babysitting is another way to get money from home. Word-of-mouth recommendations are an excellent way to begin babysitting, but there are also several websites where you may promote your babysitting services for free.

Keep in mind that the majority of families prefer to care for their children at home. To make oneself more desirable to families, try obtaining appropriate qualifications like CPR and first aid.

☐ **Test websites.**

Another approach to earn money from home is to use services that pay you for your feedback on how well a particular website performs. In most situations, you must pass a test to be accepted, and you get paid for each exam you complete. You may even be able to earn additional cash by participating in a video discussion with the customer after passing the test.

☐ **Perform data entry.**

If you have quick, accurate typing skills, you might be interested in working from home by doing online data entry. These occupations are usually easy to complete online and can provide a constant income. Data entry jobs may require utilizing a word processor or spreadsheets to enter text and numbers in a specified order and format.

☐ **Work as a freelance writer.**

To improve their search engine performance, companies of all sizes frequently require high-quality content. If you have strong writing skills, this could be a good option. If you don't currently have an online portfolio of published writing, you may volunteer to write a few pieces for free to help establish one.

Related: How To Become A Freelance Writer: A Guide To Getting Started.

☐ **Offer proofreading services.**

If you have an eye for detail and a solid understanding of proper spelling and punctuation, you might want to consider working from home as a freelance proofreader. If you are not an accomplished writer or editor, you can consider enrolling in a proofreading school to gain credibility with potential clients. You might sell your skills to clients on your own or look for organizations that use full-time, remote proofreaders.

☐ **Rent out a room in your house.**

Listing a spare bedroom on a vacation rental website might provide easy home-based income. If you do, make sure to verify your local property usage rules, get the appropriate insurance, and dedicate effort to keeping your property and home clean. To maintain high occupancy rates, consider offering your home on numerous websites and promoting it on social media.

## Price Your Products and Services

The price you charge for your product or service is one of the most essential business decisions you'll make. Setting an excessively high or cheap pricing will, at best, hinder your company's growth. At worst, it could have major implications for your sales and cash flow.

If you are beginning a business, thoroughly evaluate your pricing plan before you begin. Established businesses can increase their profitability by conducting regular pricing assessments.

When choosing your prices, ensure that the price and sales levels you choose will allow your firm to be successful. You should also consider how your product or service compares to that of your competitors.

This article teaches you how to create a pricing plan and calculate your costs and pricing to ensure your business is profitable. It also looks at various pricing strategies and how to change your prices.

- The distinction between cost and value
- Covering both fixed and variable costs.
- Cost-plus versus value-based pricing.
- How to Create a Pricing Strategy
- Various pricing approaches
- Increasing or decreasing prices

**The distinction between cost and value**

Understanding the difference between cost and value helps boost profitability:

The cost of your product or service is the amount you spend on producing it.

The price represents your financial compensation for supplying the goods or service. Value is what your customer thinks the product or service is worth to them.

For example, a plumber may charge $5 for travel, $5 for materials, and $30 for an hour of labor to repair a burst pipe at a customer's home. However, the value of the service to the customer, who may have water leaking throughout their home, is significantly larger than the $40 fee, thus the plumber may elect to charge a total of $100.

Pricing should be consistent with the value of the benefits that your company gives to its clients, while also taking into account the rates that your competitors charge.

To increase profitability, identify the benefits your customers receive from utilizing your product or service, as well as the factors they consider when making purchasing decisions, such as speed of delivery, convenience, or reliability.

What value do your consumers place on receiving the benefits you offer?

Wherever possible, set prices that reflect the value you offer rather than just the cost.

**Covering both fixed and variable costs.**

Every business must cover its costs in order to turn a profit. Working out your costs accurately is an important component of determining your pricing.

Divide your costs into two categories:

Fixed costs are those that are always present, regardless of how much or how little you sell, such as rent, salaries, and company fees.

Variable costs are those that rise when your sales expand, such as more raw materials, labor, and transportation.

When you set a price, it must exceed the variable cost of manufacturing your product or service. Each sale will thus contribute to meeting your fixed costs and generating profits.

For example, a car dealership must pay variable costs of $18,000 each vehicle sold as well as total fixed expenditures of $400,000 per year. If the company sells 80 automobiles each year, it will need to contribute at least $5,000 per car ($400,000 divided by 80) to prevent losing money.

Using this approach, you may evaluate the impact of establishing various price levels:

If the auto dealership sells cars for less than $18,000 (the variable cost per car), it loses money on each one sold and does not cover any of its fixed expenditures.

Selling 80 automobiles for $18,000 results in a $400,000 loss per year because none of the fixed expenditures are paid.

Selling automobiles at $23,000 breaks even, if the intended 80 cars are sold (80 contributions of $5,000 per car = $400,000, i.e. the fixed expenditures).

Selling automobiles for $24,000 results in a profit, if 80 cars are sold.

If more or fewer than 80 cars are sold, profits are proportionally higher or lower.

**Cost-plus versus value-based pricing.**
There are two main ways to price your products and services: cost-plus and value-based pricing. The ideal option relies on your type of business, what motivates your clients to buy, and the nature of your competition.

Cost-plus pricing

This calculates the cost of manufacturing your product or service and adds the amount required to generate a profit. This is typically given as a percentage of the cost.

It is often better suited to organizations that deal with high volumes or operate in price-competitive markets.

However, cost-plus pricing overlooks your image and market position. Hidden expenditures are easily overlooked, therefore your true profit per transaction is frequently smaller than you realize.

Value-based pricing

This focuses on the price you believe clients are willing to pay for the benefits your company provides.

Value-based pricing is based on the strength of the benefits you can demonstrate to clients.

If you have clearly defined benefits that provide you an advantage over your competition, you can charge based on the value you provide to customers. While this method can be extremely successful, it can alienate potential customers who are just motivated by price and attract new competitors.

**How to Create a Pricing Strategy**

You must select whether to utilize cost-plus or value-based pricing.

It's critical to understand what your competitors offer and how much they charge. If you call your competitors and ask for a quote, you can use this information as a guideline.

It's probably a bad idea to set your prices excessively high or low without a valid justification. If you price too cheaply, you will waste your profit. If you price too high, you will lose clients unless you can provide them with something they cannot find elsewhere.

It is equally crucial to consider how others perceive your product or service. In many markets, a high price helps to the perception of your product as having superior value. This may inspire customers to buy from you, but it may also dissuade price-conscious shoppers.

It can be beneficial to charge various pricing to different consumers, such as those who make repeat purchases or buy add-on or related products, as a way of thanking them for their loyalty. Keep in mind that consumers that are expensive to serve will be less lucrative unless you charge them more money. One-time sales could cost you more than repeat business.

You can also employ pricing strategies to entice clients. See the following section for information on various pricing strategies.

Whatever rates you choose, make sure they cover your costs and generate a profit. See the page in this handbook that discusses fixed and variable costs.

**Various pricing approaches**

Different strategies can help you gain more consumers and increase earnings.

Discounting

Offering specially reduced prices might be an effective technique. This could be a clearance price to sell old stock, a discount for purchasing numerous items of the same or similar type, or bulk discounts to promote larger orders. You should be able to increase these profits by lowering costs.

But take care. If you discount too heavily, clients may question your full-rate pricing or perceive you as a low-cost choice, making it difficult to charge full-rate prices in the future.

Odd value pricing

Using the retailer's strategy of selling things for $9.99 instead of $10 can be beneficial if pricing is an important factor in customers' purchasing decisions. Some buyers see strange value prices like these as more appealing.

Loss Leader

This entails selling a product for a low, or even loss-making price. Although you may not earn from this offering, you may attract clients who will purchase other, more profitable products.

Skimming

You can charge a premium for your one-of-a-kind product or service. This is known as skimming, so be sure what you're selling is unique.

Otherwise, you may just price yourself out of the market if there is serious competition.

Penetration

This is the opposite of skimming: starting low and acquiring market share before competitors catch up. Once you establish a devoted customer base, you should be able to find ways to increase prices later.

**Increasing or decreasing prices**

There will be instances when you need to adjust your pricing. However, before making any price changes, you should consider the influence on business profitability.

There are two crucial questions you must answer:

- How will the price adjustment affect the amount of sales?
- What will be the impact on profit per sale?

**Increasing prices**

Increasing prices can boost your profitability even if your sales volume falls.

If you raise your pricing, always explain why you are doing so. You might use the pricing change to re-emphasize the benefits you provide. A decent explanation might also help you build a relationship with a consumer.

There are also techniques to conceal price increases. Consider introducing new, higher-priced products or services and discontinuing older, cheaper ones. Alternatively, cut specifications and costs while maintaining the same price.

However, be mindful that hiding price rises may result in negative reactions from customers if they discover what you are doing.

**Lowering prices**

Never take the choice to cut prices carelessly. Low costs frequently coincide with poor-quality service; is this the image you want to project for your business?

Concentrate on increasing profits rather than lowering prices to increase sales. In most cases, your clients choose to buy from you based on the benefits you provide, as well as your price. It is unusual for a selection to be made entirely based on pricing.

## Real-World Examples: Converting Knowledge into Income

Here are a few ways to turn knowledge into wealth:

**Become an expert consultant or independent advisor:** Use your extensive understanding of a specific sector, issue, or talent to give consulting services, training, or advise to organizations and individuals who require your expertise.

**Create and sell instructional content:** Create ebooks, online courses, videos, or other instructional products to share your knowledge and experience with paying consumers. This enables you to monetize your knowledge at scale.

**License your intellectual property:** If you have created patents, copyrights, or other valuable intellectual property, you can license it to businesses or individuals who want to use it, resulting in continuing royalties.

**Launch a knowledge-based business:** Make use of your particular knowledge to develop a product or service that helps customers solve an issue. This could include creating a software application, starting a niche newspaper, or providing a unique service.

**Become a public speaker or writer:** Share your expertise through speaking engagements, media appearances, or published papers and books. This establishes you as an expert in your subject and may lead to consultancy, advice, or other income opportunities.

**Teach or offer training:** Share your knowledge by teaching classes, running workshops, or offering professional development training, whether in person or online.

**Invest in knowledge assets:** Use your expertise to make sound investments in stocks, real estate, and other assets that will appreciate in value over time.

The idea is to discover the areas in which your knowledge is most valuable and then figure out how to effectively monetize it. Continuously developing your knowledge and skills can lead to new wealth-generating opportunities over time.

# CHAPTER 6:

# CREATING VALUABLE CONTENT

## Writing Blogs, Articles, and E-books

☐ **Writing Blogs**

What constitutes a blog post?

A blog post is a piece of content published on a blog that usually includes text, photographs, videos, or other multimedia elements. Blog postings can be of various lengths and formats, covering a wide range of topics. They are frequently informal, conversational, and engaging, offering information, thoughts, opinions, or amusement to the blog's readership. Blog entries can have a variety of aims, such as teaching, entertaining, motivating, or fostering conversation.

**How to Write a Blog Post in 13 Steps**

- Brainstorm blog themes.
- Use keyword research to refine your theme.

- Define your audience.
- Develop an ordered outline.
- Write compelling content.
- Create an intriguing headline
- Select a blog template.
- Choose a blog domain name.
- Choose appropriate photos.
- Implement calls to action.
- Optimize for SEO
- Edit and publish your blog posts.
- Promote the finished article.

- **Generate blog topics**

When writing a blog post, whether you're guest posting for someone else or writing for your own blog, you should address themes that are valuable to your readers and align with both their and your own interests. Rather than attempting to pick the perfect topic straight away, begin by writing down many thoughts that occur to mind.

There are various locations to explore for new topic ideas:

Browse other blogs in your niche and conduct competitor analysis. If you're establishing a trip blog, for example, search "travel blog" to discover what your competitors are writing about.

Use the AI technologies at your disposal to generate topic ideas.

Use Google Trends to find out what topics are popular.

Look for current events and news stories relevant to your field.

Browse online courses like Udemy, Skillshare, and LinkedIn Learning to discover what people are interested in learning about.

When you come across any interesting ideas online, consider the several approaches you may take to those topics. Consider the different ways you might experiment with topic ideas to create something that is not only trendy and relevant, but also unique and fresh. You should also consider keeping your blog post up to date, which means presenting current data and statistics on the issue.

Let's imagine you want to write about chocolate chip cookies. Depending on your target demographic and the possibilities for website traffic, you might consider a few alternative approaches:

A how-to piece that teaches readers how to accomplish something in clearly arranged steps (e.g., "How to Bake Chocolate Chip Cookies from Scratch")

A curated list that provides a series of recommendations for your viewers (for example, "The Top Chocolate Chip Cookie Recipes").

A post with recommendations and advice from experts, as well as resources. (e.g., "Tips for Making Homemade Chocolate Chip Cookies Extra Gooey" )

A blog article that defines a term or topic (e.g., "What Are No-Bake Chocolate Chip Cookies?").

A top trends post that highlights what is currently popular (for example, "The Best Chocolate Chip Cookie Recipes From This Year").

A personal or business update that allows you to reveal something new or previously unknown (e.g., "My New Chocolate Chip Cookie Recipe Revealed")

Start brainstorming with these excellent blog ideas, and for further advice, see our professional guide to starting a blog. You can also ask folks close to you for input on your ideas, or reach out to a larger audience to obtain their perspectives.

- **Conduct keyword research to narrow down your topic.**

Keyword research is an essential component of crafting a blog post. This important SEO tactic serves as a marker to determine which terms you can potentially rank well for in specific web searches.

Once you've decided on a topic for your blog post, before you begin writing, you'll need to determine the likelihood of its success on search engine result pages—which ultimately means gaining more eyes on your material. To succeed, undertake keyword research to identify the most relevant questions for your topic.

Various keyword research tools might help you find keywords for your own content. If you're new to blogging, you should probably start with free resources like Ubersuggest and Google Keyword Planner. After that, you may want to consider upgrading to more powerful tools such as SEMrush or Ahref.

When undertaking keyword research, remember that the more detailed the phrase, the more it will match your audience's intent. Broader terms, on the other hand, have larger search volumes, which means that more people look for them every month.

Consider the benefits of using a larger word, such as "chocolate chip cookies," rather than a more specific phrase, such as "how to make chocolate chip cookies." Selecting the appropriate keywords entails striking a balance between high search volume and high intent.

Once you've decided on your keywords, you can utilize them to determine the structure of your content. Google those phrases to see whether publications have effectively targeted the same keywords, and then spend some time reading their content. This will serve as inspiration for your own post, both in terms of content and structure. Don't forget to draw on your own experience as an entrepreneur or writer when deciding what to write about.

- **Define your audience.**

Now that you've decided what you'll be writing about, you need to figure out who you're writing for. Anticipating who will read your postings will allow you to develop material that is fascinating, engaging, relevant, and shareable.

Of course, your target audience is primarily determined by the type of blog you write. If you operate a baking blog, you're probably writing for a group of people who enjoy baking and are looking for recipe ideas. More specifically, if you operate a healthy baking blog, you'll be writing for folks who enjoy baking but want to make their recipes healthier. It's critical to keep these details in mind when creating content, as the goal is to generate articles that resonate powerfully with readers.

So, how do you identify your audience in the first place? Start by reviewing the other blogs in your field. Consider who they appear to be writing for, and the assumptions they make about their readers' interests and lifestyles. For example, you may see that the majority of the blogs target a specific gender or age range.

You can also use internet forums to identify the most often asked questions by your target audience, or visit Facebook groups to learn about the topics they enjoy or discuss. This will assist you in developing content that piques their attention, arouses their curiosity, and answers their queries.

Whether you're launching a book blog, a fashion blog, a vacation blog, or something else, you should define your target audience first.

- **Prepare a structured outline.**

The key to understanding how to write a blog post is to conduct extensive research and planning before writing the article itself. After choosing a topic and blog format, you'll need to create a mold for your content. Creating an outline is crucial because it guarantees that your article has a solid basis on which to build as you compose your blog post.

**Begin by generating subheadings,** which serve as the foundation for an orderly outline and will be used to place your paragraphs of text. These short yet powerful chunks of material let you break down your post into bite-sized sections, making it easier to write and more consumable for readers.

If you're creating a step-by-step tutorial or a list of tips, begin by clearly identifying all of the major points, as shown in the example below:

Outline: How to make chocolate chip cookies from scratch.
1. Gather the ingredients.
2. Mix and knead dough.
3. Line a baking sheet with parchment paper.
4. Scoop mounds of dough onto the baking sheet.
5. Bake at 350 °F.

Include bulleted notes in your introduction and under each subheading. This will help you organize your important points.

If you get stuck, utilize one of these blog post templates to help you through the outline process.

- **Create compelling content**.

Turning something you enjoy and know a lot about into blog entries is an excellent way to attract readers: they'll come for the knowledge, but they'll stay for your genuine perspective and firsthand experiences.

Hanna Kimelblat, a blogger and growth marketing expert at Wix

Now that you've sketched out your blog post, you can start typing (or use AI to write it). Keep in mind that, like many other sorts of writing, blog entries usually consist of three basic components: an introduction, body text, and conclusion.

Let's start with the introduction. In the opening few phrases of your article, you should have your readers' attention. Begin with a pertinent quotation or statistic, a brief tale, or an interesting fact. Then, set the tone for the piece by providing a brief description of what you plan to discuss in the body content. This gives your audience a reason to keep reading.

Next, enter the body text. In your outline, these are the bullet points under each subsection. This is the meat of your blog post, so make it clear and interesting. Avoid fluff and repetition and instead provide deep value by sharing your knowledge, research, and thoughts.

A conclusion isn't always necessary—in fact, our blog rarely employs one—but it can be handy for narrative or closing up a lengthy essay. You can connect your major points with a brief bulleted list or by giving some concluding remarks in a few phrases. Whatever the situation, you'll want to end on an intriguing note.

At this point, you'll also want to examine your writing style, which is typically decided by your blog audience. If you're writing for a professional business audience, you might want to try a more official writing style; if you're writing for bakers, something more light and entertaining may be the ideal option. Consider your tone as well; blogs, including formal corporate ones, are intended to foster contact and conversation. Make sure your tone is appropriate for your writing style and readership, but also use welcome and uplifting language whenever possible.

Other key concepts to consider during the content production process are:

**Viscosity** refers to how easily a reader can understand and flow through a piece of material. It is similar to the "fluidity" of the writing and how easily thoughts and information are transferred to the reader. High viscosity in writing suggests that the content is dense, convoluted, and difficult to read, whereas low viscosity indicates that the writing is clear, succinct, and simple to understand.

**Rhythm** is the pattern of stressed and unstressed syllables, sentence patterns, and word flow that contribute to the text's melodic or harmonious nature. The cadence and beat give the writing a sense of movement, making it more engaging and memorable.

**Creativity** is the ability to express oneself imaginatively and inventively using the written word. It entails creating interesting stories, poems, essays, or other written content using one's distinct perspective, original ideas, emotion, pathos, and artistic flare. Creative writing allows writers to explore their thoughts, emotions, and observations in a unique and expressive way. Storytelling is an essential component of producing a blog article and should not be overlooked.

**Sentence and clause structure** are key grammatical features that determine the construction of sentences in English. They decide how to organize words (verbs, adjectives), sentences, and clauses in order to convey meaning and ensure communication clarity.

Understanding sentence and clause form is critical to good writing and communication.

**Create an enticing headline.**

When creating a blog article, you'll need more than just great information; you'll also want a compelling headline. A fantastic headline entices readers and improves your blog design, increasing the likelihood that they will click on your content in the first place.

Learning how to write an engaging blog title does not have to be difficult. All you need to do is remember the following: be clear, explicit, and provide an answer or solution.

Writing a compelling headline also relies on your ability to put yourself in the shoes of your target audience. Use the title to promise readers that your blog post will deliver useful information that will benefit them in some way, such as gratifying their intellectual curiosity, teaching them something new, or assisting them in solving a problem. This increases the likelihood that they will click on your content and read it. Just don't go overboard, and avoid clickbait, which is the practice of drafting a hyperbolic headline in order to entice readers to click on an article.

Here are some samples of headlines that we are very proud of, to give you a broad concept for your own content.

**Create a powerful free landing page in less than an hour.**

20 Best Time Management Apps for Organizing Your Life.

How to Design an A+ School Website (with Examples)

Make a Change: Using Photography to Raise Awareness.

If you need inspiration to get started, use this blog post title generator.

- **Select a blog template.**

Writing your blog post may be your top focus, but you should also present it in an appealing manner. Having an article with a great visual appeal is essential for striking the proper note with your viewers. The best approach to personalize your blog's style is to begin with a free blog template.

All of these blog layouts were created by professional designers and may be fully customized to fit your site's messaging and tone.

Check out the blog examples for inspiration on how others have transformed the templates into visually stunning, content-rich powerhouses.

If you're writing a blog on organic foods, for example, having a natural color palette for your site will help to set the tone for the themes you'll be covering. The same color palette should be used for your blog logo and social networking sites.

- **Choose a blog domain name**.

To ensure that viewers find your well-crafted blog, host it on your domain site URL. When it comes to naming your blog, you might get inspiration from a blog name generator and see if the domain name is accessible.

Consider how your blog and domain name relate to the blog post subjects you will address. Make sure your blog's name accurately portrays its persona, topic, and specialization.

Once you've decided on a name, choose a domain name (also known as a URL, such as www.wix.com). Typically, your domain name will be the same or quite similar to the name of your blog.

- **Choose appropriate photos**.

Similarly, you should supplement your blog article with a few high-quality photographs that illustrate your key points. It is critical that your images provide value to the subject, rather than acting as placeholders. Pay close attention to your featured image—it will be the prominent visual underneath your blog's title and what people will see when they browse your articles from the homepage. Infographics are also excellent for highlighting key ideas or key statistics in blog entries.

Consider incorporating videos within your blog posts; the ideal ones are those you made to match the video's theme and intent, but you can also use third-party movies to increase the user experience and engagement rates on your articles.

Wix allows you to add a professional photo gallery to individual posts and integrate your own images into your articles. You can also select media assets from Wix, Shutterstock, and Unsplash straight in your site's editor.

- **Implement calls to action.**

In the same way that a blog is intended to inform people about specific topics, it can also serve as a crucial tool for motivating readers to take action. This encompasses everything from following your blog to making a purchase.

This element is known as a CTA, or call-to-action, and it appears as an embedded link or button that outlines your goal in an appealing way. The most typical call-to-action examples for blogs are "Subscribe," "Download our ebook," and "Sign up."

CTAs can help you convert website traffic into interaction and, ultimately, profit. While your immediate goal is to gain more readers, you may want to consider monetizing your blog in the future.

- **Optimize for SEO**

An effective SEO strategy for bloggers includes optimizing your content both before and after you write the blog article. This entails not only conducting keyword research before beginning the outline phase (as indicated in step 3), but also employing those keywords to refine your final content.

This starts with using relevant keywords throughout your post. Let's imagine you've decided to target the keyword "business strategies." Use this identical phrase in your headline, body text, and one or two subheadings if it's a good fit.

Next, add this keyword to your metadata. This is the preview text you'll see for every article on Google, and it comprises a title (known as the meta title) and a brief description (the meta description). You should also include the keywords in the URL of your article and the alt text of your blog posts' photos. Use these SEO elements to improve your blog's overall performance. Finally, ensure that you understand how long a blog post should be in order to rank well.

- **Edit and publish your blog article.**

With so many frequent blogging mistakes out there, you'll want to double-check your piece for grammatical problems, spelling issues, repetition, and any other unprofessional content. Furthermore, ensure that your ideas flow smoothly through each section, conveying a clear and intended message to readers. This complete blog post checklist includes information on other important areas of blogging.

As part of your editing and fact-checking process before publication, we recommend having a friend or colleague review your blog post. Direct them to check for any inconsistencies or ambiguities. It's also crucial to prioritize quality over quantity in order to keep your readers interested and develop credibility. When you're satisfied with your writing, hit the publish button.

- **Promote the final item.**

Once you've written and published the blog article, take the required measures to ensure it's read. Email and social media marketing are two of the most effective strategies to promote your blog article and attract visitors.

Email is still one of the most reliable marketing channels since it allows you to communicate directly with your target audience. This very efficient digital marketing method is sending personalized emails to prospective users in the hopes of converting them into loyal fans. If you want to get started, this strong email marketing service can help you send personalized newsletters for your site.

Sharing your content on social media, in addition to emails, can be very effective. If you want to reach a huge audience, promote your blog on Facebook or Instagram, which have the largest and most diverse user communities.

Whatever channels you use, make sure to regularly engage with your fans on a daily basis. This will ensure that you not only write a wonderful blog post, but that others read it as well.

Want to truly get your blog off the ground? To get started, check out our online course, Build Your Own Blog

.

**How to structure a blog article checklist.**
**Headline:** straightforward, snappy, and relevant, with keywords where applicable for SEO.

**Introduction:** grabs the reader, answers search intent when relevant, and defines the blog's objective and major point.

Subheadings divide text into consumable and legible pieces, following a logical flow.

**Body:** gives useful information while supporting views with examples, statistics, and other evidence, conversational tone.

Visuals contain pertinent images, infographics, or films that boost comprehension and reader engagement.

**Engagement:** fosters reader involvement (comments and shares).

Editing: checks for grammatical and spelling mistakes; edited for coherence and style; fact checked.

**SEO:** incorporates relevant keywords naturally, responds to search intent

Readability: utilize consistent font and formatting, brief sentences.

Links: contains internal and external links for more context.

Include social sharing icons and shareable content. Review the post before and after publication.

☐ **Writing articles.**
- Define what your article will be about.

Unless you're writing just for the sake of writing (which isn't a bad thing, I promise you), you must have a reason for creating an article. So, the first step is to be as explicit about that goal as possible. Your piece need a primary point around which everything else revolves; the stronger it is, the less likely you are to veer off course during the writing process.

Assume you're drafting an article to market your incredible new product, Product X. I'm sure you'd have a lot to say about Product X, but without a clear focus, your post may quickly become a string of loosely connected views about your product that don't add anything to the reader's knowledge.

However, if you decide that your post will be about "How Product X is a Gamechanger for Y Industry", it will now have a clear purpose: to educate readers on the unique benefits or impact that your product will have on a specific industry. This provides you a clear path to follow while planning and composing the essay.

A working title might be an excellent method to outline the parameters of your piece. "How Product X Is a Gamechanger for Y Industry" is a nice working title. Alternatively, creating a logline or quick description of your content can help with this. The aim is to be more clear about what you're writing and why you're doing it before you begin.

- Be clear about your audience.

I'm calling this 'Step Two', but it's something you should keep in mind as you work on your essay. Who is just as important as what and why, and it can act as a helpful guide for you while you write. To put it simply: who are you writing for? Who is your 'target audience'? How old are they? What is their educational and professional background? What industry do they belong to? How much do they presumably already know about the topic of your article? What purpose does your piece serve for them?

This is not an entire list, but these are the types of questions you should consider before getting started. If you are writing for an organization, your internal marketing/communications team may be able to provide you with specific answers to these questions. In any event, it's critical to consider this and have a broad grasp of who your target audience is while writing your essay.

Putting yourself in the shoes of your intended audience helps guide you through everything from article structure to language and tone.

- Create an outline.

Knowing what your post will be about and who it is intended for offers you a starting point, but your content must first be structured. And this leads us to an important part of the planning process: the outline.

An outline helps you focus while writing and clarifies the eventual consequence for your viewers.

There are no hard and fast rules for creating an outline. It could be as simple as a list of subtopics/subheadings or a brief paragraph-long summary of the full article. Mindmaps could potentially be a useful outlining tool. Depending on the length and complexity of the piece, I prefer to use a list of subheadings or a series of bullet points with 1-2 line summaries of each subheading.

When arranging your post, it's always a good idea to break it down into sections. An essay with numerous clear subheadings is naturally suited to this type of organization. Even if your content is free-flowing and lacks precise subheadings, it's a good idea to break it down into broad sections while outlining it.

At the most fundamental level of structure, your piece should include an introduction and a conclusion. The opening can be as brief as one paragraph or as long as several paragraphs and should establish the background for the post, including what it will be about and what the audience's primary takeaways will be. To use a marketing word, your opening should entice your visitors to "opt in" to read the entire piece!

Your conclusion can highlight the main ideas or takeaways from your piece and should, ideally, refer back to the opening. For example, if your introduction states that your article is answering a specific question (say, "How Technology X is going to revolutionize the retail industry"), your conclusion should briefly reflect on the answers provided by your article - either by summarizing

the key points discussed or reinforcing the broad ideas.
- Write! (And Review)

Needless to say, after all that planning, you must eventually start writing!

Pacing is important while writing a long article. Go through each segment, taking breaks in between to refresh your thoughts and examine what you've written.

The previous three processes we've covered in this writing and reviewing process are your guardian angels. Always keep in mind the topic of your essay and your intended audience. And keep to your outline.

(Quick note: if you want to edit or add something substantial to the article while writing, go back to your outline and make the change there first, so you can see how the changes effect the general structure of your essay).

When you get caught up in the flow of writing, it's easy to drift away from the main topic or idea of your essay, or to forget who you're writing for. Revisiting your planning process will keep you on target.

While writing, try to make the transition between sections as smooth as possible, so that they feel like they are part of a whole rather than a collection of separate mini-articles. One method to accomplish this is to begin each section by referencing the preceding one. Alternatively, start each section by returning to the article's main theme or topic. In fact, it's a good idea to reinforce your main point/topic throughout the post (at least once in each section).

- Prepare visual elements (if needed)

This is an optional step, as your article may not have any visual elements. But it is still an important one.

Visual components, such as images, photographs, illustrations, infographics, embedded videos, and so on, can significantly improve the quality of your post. At the very least, they make your article visually appealing. In the event of a long piece, they help break up the long walls of text, making it more readable. More importantly, they can highlight the arguments you're making throughout the article. For example, remember the cheat-sheet I included at the beginning of this article?

Of course, whether or not to add visual elements in your piece, as well as how many, is determined by your capacity to generate or source visuals. If you're writing for an organization, you'll most certainly have access to visual designers who can assist you here.

If you include visual elements, you should absolutely work on getting them ready once you've finished your first draft. But it's absolutely not too early to start thinking about them at the outline stage.

- Review and edit.

The work does not cease after you have written the final word. Once you've completed your initial draft, go over your piece again for a thorough evaluation.

One of the first things you should do is proofread your content for grammar issues. You can trust your own judgment or utilize a tool like Grammarly. This is a necessary quality check for anyone creating an article.

Make sure your piece is appropriately arranged, with each section flowing easily into the next. If your article incorporates visual elements, check their arrangement to ensure that they match the content and improve the piece's readability and visual attractiveness.

While reviewing your post, consider the audience you identified during the planning process and put yourself in their position. Will the article be helpful to them? Are the points being conveyed clearly understood? Would readers find the article engaging? If not, is there anything you can do to make the content more valuable to the readers and/or enjoyable to read? While reviewing, remember the main topic and idea of your piece and make sure you've stayed on course. Perhaps there is a sentence or paragraph that is off-topic? Or is there a point that might be changed to better reflect the fundamental topic?

If time allows, it's a good idea to get the article reviewed by someone else. If you're writing for an organization, a coworker or team member (whether a peer, supervisor, or subordinate) would make an excellent reviewer. Someone who represents or has a thorough understanding of your target demographic might likewise be an excellent choice. If your piece is intended for a large readership, or the general public, even having a friend or family member read it can provide significant input!

A few other points to bear in mind:

If you incorporate any facts, figures, or statistics from an external source, make sure to acknowledge it in your post and, if possible, include a link to it. If your piece is an academic work, you must add citations in any situation.

I haven't included SEO (Search Engine Optimization) in this work, but it is a crucial consideration for any item published online. If you're writing for a company, in-house SEO/content specialists can assist you optimize your post before it's published. However, if you want to work on making your content SEO-friendly yourself, try to obtain a list of keywords relevant to your main topic/idea from your internal team. Alternatively, you can use a variety of free and paid keyword research tools, such as SEMRush, Answer the Public, BuzzSumo, and Google Keyword Planner. However, SEO is a broad discipline that you should generally focus on after you've honed your skills in other areas of article writing.

### ☐ Writing E-books

What is an ebook?

An ebook, short for 'electronic book,' is a digital version of a printed book that can be read on devices such as computers, tablets, and smartphones. Ebooks are valuable marketing assets that contain several digital 'pages' that provide information to the reader. Furthermore, they are frequently bundled as PDF documents, allowing readers to share them.

**How to Write an Ebook?**

- Choose a topic that is relevant to your audience's needs.
- Conduct research.
- Outline each chapter of your ebook.
- Break down each chapter as you write.
- Create your ebook.
- Use the correct colors.
- Incorporate visuals.
- Highlight quotations or statistics.
- Place suitable calls to action throughout your ebook.

- Convert it to a PDF.
- Make a separate landing page for your ebook.
- Promote your ebook and monitor its success.

Ebooks can boost your company's visibility and reputation, as well as position your brand as an industry thought leader. Despite the fact that these ebooks provide numerous benefits, they might be difficult to create at times.

Here are some tried-and-true tips for creating high-quality ebooks.

- **Choose a topic that is relevant to your audience's needs.**

Remember, the purpose of your ebook is to generate leads for your sales team, so choose a topic that will allow a prospect to easily transition from reading your ebook to speaking with your sales team.

This means that your ebook should not depart significantly from the topics covered in your existing content delivery methods.

Rather, it's an opportunity for you to go deeply into a topic you've just briefly touched on previously but that your audience is interested in learning more about.

For example, after listening to sales and customer calls here at HubSpot, I discovered that publishing ebooks is a huge barrier for our audience, who are marketers themselves. but tools to make ebook authoring easier, and I'm focusing on the right issue, which will inevitably lead to a sales discussion.

**Here are some sample ebook titles to get your creative juices going.**
X Best Practices for [Insert Industry or Topic]
An Introduction to [Insert Industry or Topic]
X Common Questions About [Insert Industry/Topic] Answered X [Insert Industry/Topic]. Learn from the best with statistics for better decision-making (X). [Insert Industry/Topic]. Experts Share Insights
Replace "x" with the appropriate number. You may also use our free Blog Topic Generator to generate more ideas. Most blog subjects are detailed enough to serve as longer-form ebook content.

- **Conduct research.**

Although you undoubtedly already know a lot about your topic, you still need to find out what your target audience wants to know and how to differentiate your ebook from others on the market.

When researching for your ebook, consider the following:

Read through previous publications on your topic to find knowledge gaps and topics for further investigation. During your study, take the time to answer any unanswered questions to make your ebook more complete and valuable.

Conduct keyword research to identify keywords and phrases relevant to the topic you're writing about. This allows you to identify trends in your subject matter and better attract users who want to learn more about it.

Collect original data and insights to set your ebook apart from other sources and establish yourself as an authority on your subject. If possible, reach out to industry experts and conduct interviews to gather unique data. You can also conduct surveys with your audience to gather statistics to support your content.

Once you've gathered all of your information, make sure it's correct and up to date. Also, keep your discoveries structured so you can readily refer back to them as you write your ebook.

Free eBook Templates

Free templates and themes to help you construct your own ebook.

- **Create an outline for each chapter of your ebook.**

The opening to your ebook should set the tone for the book's content and entice the reader.

What topics will you address in your eBook? How will the reader gain from reading it?

The ideal method to structure your ebook is to think of it as a crash course in the sales-related topic you chose.

Write effective copy.

Design an ebook.

Optimize eBooks for Lead Generation and Promotion.

- **Break down each chapter as you write.**

Start writing! Here, you can approach each chapter in the same way you would a large blog post: by breaking it down into smaller chunks or bullet points.

This allows you to write more simply and plainly, rather than utilizing complex jargon to express each idea. It's the most effective technique to educate and help readers understand the fresh information you're delivering.

Maintain a similar framework throughout each chapter, as well. This allows you to create natural transitions between each chapter, resulting in a clear progression from one to the next.

Use keywords in the title to highlight the value of your offer. Examples include adjectives like "amazing," "awesome," and "ultimate."

Maintain consistency in your format to help readers construct a mental picture and better absorb the material.

When appropriate, employ formatting such as bulleted lists, bold text, italics, and font size modifications to direct readers' attention to your most significant content or highlight specific points you want readers to remember.

- Create your eBook.
- Use the correct colors.

- **Incorporate visuals.**

Images and graphics in ebooks are difficult to get right. The key to making them work successfully is to consider them as complements to your content. Your images, whether included during or after you've completed writing the content for your ebook, should serve to highlight an important point you're making or to dissect the meaning of a concept in an easy-to-understand, visual method.

Images should not be included solely to make the ebook more visually appealing. Rather, they should be employed to help the reader understand the stuff you're discussing.

- **Highlight quotations or statistics.**

Another technique to improve your ebook is to highlight quotes or statistics inside the design. Just be sure the quotation or stat you're using actually adds value to the article.

Maintain consistent margins throughout your material, whether you're accentuating a phrase or adding an image. If your copy is consistently one-inch indented on both the left and right edges of your page, align your created elements with the same space.

**Include suitable calls to action in your ebook.**

Now that you've written and developed your content, it's time to optimize it for lead generation, re-engagement, and promotion.

Consider how you came here: you clicked on a call-to-action (CTA) in an email, a social media post, or someplace else. A call to action (CTA) is a link or visual object that entices visitors to click and arrive at a landing page where they may get further connected with your brand.

Since your ebook readers have most likely converted into leads in order to obtain your ebook, use the CTAs within your ebook to reconvert your readers and propel them further down your marketing funnel.

A CTA, for example, can direct visitors to another offer, your annual conference registration page, or even a product page. Depending on the next action, CTAs might range from an in-line rectangle to a full-page teasing the following offer.

**Convert it to a PDF.**

Once you've completed authoring your ebook, including the CTAs, it's important to convert it to the appropriate file type so it can be transferred from you to your recipient.

- **Create a landing page specifically for your ebook.**

Your ebook should be available to download from a landing page on your website. A landing page is a web page that promotes/describes your offer and includes a form where visitors must enter their contact information in order to view your ebook. This is how you can turn visitors into business leads, which your sales team can then follow up on.

- **Promote your ebook and monitor its performance.**

Once your landing page is complete, you can utilize the destination URL to promote your ebook through your marketing channels. Here are five ways you can accomplish this:

Promote your new eBook on your website. For example, include a CTA or a link to your offer's landing page on your resources page or even your homepage.

Promote your ebook on your blog. Consider posting an excerpt from your ebook as a blog post. Alternatively, produce a separate blog piece on the same topic as your ebook and include a link to it at the end of your post with a call-to-action to encourage them to continue learning. (Note: This blog post is an excellent example of how to market an offer you developed through a blog post.)

Send a segmented email to contacts who have expressed interest in receiving offers from your firm.

Use paid advertising and co-marketing partnerships to promote your ebook to a new audience.

Share posts on social media with a link to your eBook. You can also improve social sharing by including social media share buttons in your ebook.

After you've launched and marketed your material through your marketing channels, you'll need marketing analytics to track the success of your ebook. For example, landing page analytics can tell you how many people downloaded your ebook or how many of those downloaders become opportunities and customers for your company.

**how to publish an ebook**

Publishing an ebook can be an excellent approach to spread your message or information to a larger audience. Here's a step-by-step guide for publishing an ebook:

- Convert to eBook format

Converting your ebook to the correct format is required to ensure compatibility with your readers' devices. It allows you to add responsive design components while preserving the layout of your book. It gives a uniform reading experience across multiple platforms, extending the reach and accessibility of your ebook.

- Select a publishing platform.

When deciding on a platform, consider reach, royalty rates, distribution channels, simplicity of use, and your target audience's preferences. Depending on the specialization or target demographic of your ebook, you may want to look into regional or specialized platforms.

- Create an account and upload your eBook.

Sign up for an account on your preferred platform. Provide the relevant information, such as your name, address, and payment information, if applicable.

Once you've created an account, follow the platform's instructions to upload your ebook file and cover design. Ensure that the files adhere to the platform's formatting and size specifications. You will also need to provide the book's title, author name, description, and categories or genres. These details help users find and understand your ebook.

- Set pricing and royalties.

Determine the price for your ebook. This controls the amount of revenue you can make from each sale. By establishing the correct pricing, you can keep your ebook competitive in the market while increasing your earnings.

Once you've determined your price, you'll want to calculate your royalty rates, which are the percentage of the book's price that you get as the author or publisher for each sale.

Different ebook publishing platforms give different royalty arrangements, so it's crucial to understand the rates and terms they offer. Setting royalties allows you to calculate and estimate your earnings from each transaction.

You might also want to consider making your ebook available for free.

Although it will not earn direct income for your firm, it will increase exposure and attract a larger readership, resulting in word-of-mouth promotion and maybe increased future sales. Furthermore, it offers the potential to create leads and build an email list for future involvement.

- Preview and publish.

Before publishing, preview your ebook to check it looks as intended and that there are no errors or formatting problems. Once you're satisfied, press the publish button to make your ebook available for purchase.

Keep in mind that the processes outlined above are basic suggestions, and the actual uploading process may differ depending on the platform you choose to publish your ebook with.

## Producing Engaging Videos and Webinars

Engagement.
What a straight-laced, one-dimensional way to explain how your audience reacts to videos.

This word is far better at describing what video artists really want participation.

When your audience starts contributing to your video content, you'll notice far more than just views and clicks. You will notice:

Longer viewing times per video: People pay attention longer and watch the entire film because they are emotionally invested.

More detailed comments: When someone takes the time to convey their own thoughts and feelings about a topic, you know they're really interested in it.

Various traffic sources: Your video's traffic is coming in from a variety of sites. That suggests your viewers are spreading your films like crazy.

Engaging video content attracts and holds the audience's attention, and it has the ability to spark a chain reaction of reactions that includes your brand.

## 7 Tips for Making Engaging Videos

These seven tips apply to anyone, whether you're a marketer trying to improve your content marketing strategy with an explanation video or a content creator looking to increase your social media game.

Here's how to make the most engaging videos, get more video views, and connect with your audience.

- Create material that is relevant to your readers.

Understanding your target audience is an essential part of creating interesting videos. To effectively engage your audience, you must delve deeply into their habits, challenges, and preferences.

Metrics are important in this process because they provide key data that allows you to customize your content to your target audience. The more you learn about them, the more prepared you will be to develop videos that speak to their needs and interests.

Your video screenplay should be so tailored to your audience's perspective that it appears as if you're reading their thoughts. When viewers come upon a video that speaks directly to their internal dialogues, it fosters a strong connection and sense of relevancy.

Every video marketer hopes for the "Aha! This is for me" moment. This 'Mind-reading' strategy has been used in marketing for decades, with classic examples including the Tupperware commercials of the 1920s, which struck a deep chord with their target demographic by aligning with their objectives and goals.

- Write video scripts based on customer research.

You can find these words by conducting consumer surveys, reading reviews, or simply conversing with individuals in your audience.

Use compelling pictures and visuals.

We are all suckers for beautiful graphics. It is not our fault. We are hardwired that way. The human brain can digest visuals 60,000 times faster than words. We are, by nature, overly fixated on our visual environment.

In the age of AI, you can still create "wow" videos without ever picking up a camera. There are billions of stock photos, films, and animations available, and you can use programs like DALL-E 3 to create graphics with unsettling ease.

You can also use a free AI video creator, such as Synthesia, to create training films, explainer videos, marketing videos, or lesson videos including AI actors and voices.

So, what qualifies a visual as "striking"?

Over the years, we've discovered that panoramic shots, breathtaking drone fly-bys, and stunning photography have a place in video content creation; however, they must be relevant to your theme in order to be effective.

To keep your readers engaged, you must provide a reason for showcasing whatever photos you want to include.

Consider how you may utilize visuals to make your script more impactful. Blend animations, motion graphics, dynamic transitions, and kinetic typography. Remember, you can use colors, contrasts, and color grading to elicit moods or emotional responses.

- Tell a tale through your video.

Storytelling is a fundamental aspect of human nature, deeply embedded in our history and psychology. The earliest recorded story dates back roughly 30,000 years and was discovered on the walls of the Chauvet cave in France, demonstrating the everlasting essence of storytelling.

This intrinsic desire for stories is more than just a historical reality; it is ingrained in our brain structure. Hearing a narrative, for example, can raise cerebral activity by fivefold, according to MRI scans that show how different words excite different brain regions.

- Using storytelling in marketing, particularly video marketing, can increase engagement dramatically.

An interesting story in a marketing video has a greater impact on the audience than simply providing data or instructions.

For example, rather than employing a monotone narration to walk viewers through a product's functionalities, combining these processes into a tale structure makes the content more engaging and memorable.

- Compelling stories in explainer videos have various characteristics:

They are credible, simple to trust, and engage with.

They're relatable, bringing to mind individuals and places from your own life.

They entertain and keep you guessing what will happen next.

They impart a subtle lesson, leaving you with a message you figured out for yourself rather than being preached to.

They're remembered for their humor, their ability to inspire you, and even a trademarked line like Etsy's "Why buy boring?"

They have a distinct framework with a beginning, middle, and finish, and they typically include some tension or conflict.

This 30-second Etsy video presents a story that any parent can relate to and concludes with the brand's message, "Why buy boring?"

To increase audience engagement, try using story-based frameworks. Positioning the viewer as the "hero" of the story or employing the "hero's journey" narrative structure can be especially effective. This strategy makes the information more engaging and ensures that the message resonates strongly and remains in the viewer's memory, similar to a catchy Disney musical soundtrack.

- Evoke emotion.

When viewers feel emotionally attached to a video, they get invested in it and want a satisfactory resolution or finish.

Including emotive language in your video script is one method for creating more engaging video content. However, you should also consider the emotional reactions your audience will have to the sound, color palette, characters, atmosphere, and general style of your video.

distinct actors can evoke distinct states of mind:

The CEO can instill confidence by narrating a brand story in an explanatory video.

Employees can inspire trust by sharing work-related experiences.

A customer might participate in a video testimonial to encourage authenticity.

To get viewers' support, you can employ basic emotions such as comedy, melancholy, excitement, fear, wrath, happiness, and even playfulness. However, you can leverage a few deeper emotional ideas to guide your audience to a "that's right" reaction.

Example: "It's not my fault; the system is against me."

"It's us vs. them."

It is too late for me.

"There must be a better way."

"Others know a secret I don't."

Use tone of voice, color, relaxing music, and visual aspects to establish unforgettable emotional connections in your video content.

Hook your viewers from the beginning.

Getting a viewer's attention in the early stages of a video is critical for engagement.

According to a Microsoft study, the average human attention span has decreased dramatically and is currently only eight seconds. This rapid shift emphasizes the importance for content creators to create video material that captures their audience's attention almost instantly. Videos that fail to interest viewers during the vital initial few seconds are likely to have high drop-off rates.

Interestingly, there is no one-size-fits-all rule for the ideal length of a film.

The quality and relevance of the information are more important than its duration. Videos should be just lengthy enough to deliver the relevant information, and no longer.

On platforms such as YouTube, which has 2.2 billion monthly users, the ideal video length is often approximately 10 minutes. However, viewer engagement declines dramatically for videos longer than 60 minutes, with only 16% of viewers viewing them all the way through. Videos lasting less than 60 minutes, on the other hand, retain 62% of their viewers.

If you have a mobile audience, split down larger videos into micro-films for each topic or task. You'll force yourself to get to the point quickly and make engaging films suitable for social media networks.

- Create meaningful interactions.

360-degree views, clickable buttons, links, quizzes, checklists, and anything else that takes active participation will make viewers feel more engrossed and dedicated to finishing your film and putting it to good use.

To take it a step further, you could gamify the experience by producing scenario-based movies that allow viewers to influence how the video evolves based on what they click on.

Create interesting online video material with interactive quizzes or polls, as well as annotations or clickable links that lead viewers to related content, extra resources, or calls to action. Directly encourage viewers to write comments, ask questions, and share their ideas to promote a sense of community and involvement.

Be authentic.

A genuine personality promotes trustworthiness in your audience. Personality helps people decide whether they agree with you enough to believe what you're saying and act on it.

78% of customers believe that honest and relatable video marketing is more appealing than polished and high-quality videos.

Different personalities appeal to different types of audiences. Consider Gordon Ramsay and Jamie Oliver, two separate chefs with their own sizable followings.

What's the point? It's less about what you stand for and more about drawing an audience that shares your values.

When someone chooses your video, they begin to market it for you. They interact with your material and share your videos with others, broadening your reach and praising your work with a "Hey, this is awesome!" shoutout.

If you're making films with yourself as the presenter, include personal tales, experiences, or behind-the-scenes information. When filming, avoid an overly written or polished performance to allow your true personality to shine through. Engage with your audience through comments, feedback, and user-generated material. Make an effort to be available to everyone.

Begin creating awesome video content today.

It's time to put these recommendations into practice.

You still need to plan the next successful video.

## Expert Tips: Content that Engages Your Audience

- Know your audience.

The first step in creating content that connects is to understand who you're writing for. You must grasp your audience's needs, goals, challenges, preferences, and motivations. Buyer personas, customer surveys, social media analytics, and keyword research can all help you learn more about your target audience's demographics and behavior. Knowing your audience allows you to personalize your material to their interests, pain points, and inquiries.

- Use Clear and simple language

The second stage to creating engaging content is to employ plain and simple language. You should avoid jargon, technical phrases, and convoluted sentences that may confuse or dull your readers. You should also employ language that conveys emotion, urgency, and importance. You can use tools like Hemingway, Grammarly, and CoSchedule Headline Analyzer to assess your content's readability, grammar, and effect. Using clear and simple language will help you deliver your message more successfully and convincingly.

- Tell stories and provide examples.

The third step in creating engaging content is to relate tales and provide examples. Stories and examples are effective tools for illustrating your arguments, engaging your audience, and establishing trust and confidence. You can utilize personal tales and examples, as well as those of your customers, industry peers, or competitors. To make your information more accessible and memorable, consider using metaphors, analogies, and scenarios. Telling stories and providing examples will allow you to connect with your audience on both an emotional and cognitive level.

Provide value and solutions.

- The fourth phase in creating content that connects is to offer value and solutions.

You want to demonstrate to your audience how your material can help them solve problems, achieve their objectives, or better their circumstances. You want to concentrate on the benefits and consequences of your material, rather than just the features and specifics. You should also present your audience with concrete tips, guidance, or resources that they may apply right away. Providing value and solutions allows you to demonstrate your experience and authority.

- Use many formats and channels.

The fifth stage in creating content that connects is to use many formats and channels. You want to diversify your content portfolio in order to reach diverse sectors of your audience, accommodate different learning styles, and optimize for different platforms. You may publish your information in a variety of formats, including blog posts, videos, podcasts, infographics, ebooks, webinars, and case studies. You can also distribute your work via email, social media, search engines, and online forums. Using several forms and channels will help you gain visibility and engagement.

- Ask for feedback and interaction.

The sixth step in creating engaging content is soliciting feedback and participation. You want to encourage your audience to share their ideas, opinions, questions, and experiences with your material. You'd like to urge them to leave a comment, like, share, subscribe, or contact you. You also want to respond to their feedback and interactions in a timely and respectful manner. Asking for comments and engaging with your audience will help you establish relationships and **loyalty**.

Here's what else to consider.

This is where you can offer instances, tales, or thoughts that don't fit into any of the other areas. Anything else you'd like to add?

# CHAPTER 7:

# BUILDING A LOYAL COMMUNITY To GROW YOUR AUDIENCE.

Building a client community entails these six critical crucial steps:

- ☐ Identify Your Goals: Define your objectives first. What do you hope to achieve with your customer community? Whether it's boosting customer assistance, getting feedback, or increasing brand loyalty, having defined goals is key.
- ☐ Select the Right Platform:
  Choose a platform that is suitable for your target audience and objectives. Options include social media groups, forums, dedicated community websites, or a combination of the above. Ensure that it is user-friendly and engaging.
- ☐ Generate Relevant stuff: Provide your community with valuable stuff. Share useful articles, videos, tutorials, or hold

webinars to address your clients' interests and trouble concerns. Content is the lifeblood of your community.
- ☐ Actively participate in discussions, respond to questions and comments, and promote interaction among members. Your active participation lays the groundwork for community engagement.
- ☐ Establish explicit principles to promote positivity and respect in your community. Effective moderating is required to avoid confrontations and create a safe atmosphere for all members.
- ☐ Reward Engagement: Recognize and reward active members. Badges, unique material, or special pricing can encourage engagement and foster a sense of belonging in your group.

**How Do You Create a Community of Loyal Customers?**

Creating a network of devoted clients requires three critical strategies:

Provide exceptional value:

The foundation of loyalty is value. Consistently provide items or services that meet or exceed your customers' expectations. Make sure your offerings address their concerns or meet their demands.

**Engage Actively:**

Actively communicate with your clients across several media. Respond quickly to queries, answer issues, and solicit feedback. Demonstrate that you value your clients' thoughts and are happy to serve them.

Successful communities foster a sense of belonging among its members. Encourage relationships, create shared experiences, and celebrate successes with others to foster this emotion.

Offer exclusive bonuses to loyal consumers. This could include first access to new items or services, exclusive discounts, or personalized offers. Make them feel unique because of their loyalty.

Implement loyalty programs to reward clients for their continuous patronage. Loyalty points, tiered memberships, and exclusive event access can all help to encourage repeat business.

Personalization involves tailoring interactions with clients depending on their preferences and previous experiences with your business. Use their names, propose things based on their past purchases, and customize your communication to their preferences.

Provide instructive information that enhances your clients' life. This could take the shape of blog posts, seminars, tutorials, or educational newsletters. Becoming a valued resource increases consumer loyalty.

Encourage customers to provide feedback, ideas, and suggestions. Respond to this feedback to demonstrate that you are listening and committed to improving their experience.

Create a community for customers to connect with one another, in addition to individual encounters. This sense of community adds another layer of loyalty as customers bond over common experiences.

Consistent branding involves aligning your messaging and image. Customers who recognize and trust your brand are more likely to stay loyal.

Transparency and trust:

Build trust by being straightforward and honest in your business transactions, addressing any concerns or mistakes openly and working to resolve them in a customer-centric manner.

Surprise and delight your regular customers with unexpected incentives or tokens of appreciation. These delightful surprises can leave a lasting favorable impression.

## Excellent customer service practices.

To guarantee your consumers feel valued and get what they want from their experience with you (and without any inconvenience), consider the following:

- **Show consumers respect.**

Customers wish to feel respected and acknowledged. They do not wish to be spoken down to or disregarded. When delivering customer service, maintain a respectful and helpful tone.

- **Offer prompt assistance.**

In my experience, clients despite waiting. They frequently require immediate assistance and do not wish to be kept waiting. Set up a system that allows clients to receive assistance fast. This could include having someone answer the phone or having customer service representatives who can quickly resolve client complaints.

- **Identify solutions that genuinely suit the needs of the customers.**

Many consumers resent both waiting and having to deal with the same problem repeatedly. They want their problems answered and solutions tailored to their individual demands.

When delivering customer service, take the time to understand the customer's need and discover a solution that works for them. Resolve any issues as promptly and quickly as possible so that the consumer does not have to keep returning.

- **Communicate clearly and concisely.**

Do not confuse customers about what is going on or what they need to do. When delivering customer service, ensure that your communication is clear and understandable. This includes communicating in basic terms and avoiding jargon.

- **Be honest when things go wrong.**

Customers appreciate honesty. If something goes wrong, they want to know what happened, and they expect businesses to be open about it.

When you encounter a problem, always be honest with the customer and do not try to hide anything.

- **Prioritize client pleasure and a sense of caring.**

I've discovered that customers want to feel as if they are the only one who matters and that businesses care about them. Make sure you are focused on the specific demands of the consumer and doing everything possible to ensure their satisfaction. Demonstrate your concern for the customer's experience by going above and beyond.

- **Maintain a cheerful attitude.**

I believe that many of us can tell when someone is dissatisfied or does not want to help us; do not let this happen in your customer service. It is critical to have a cheerful attitude and demonstrate your want to assist the consumer. This can help them feel more accepted and valued.

- **Inform your team members about your business.**

Most people prefer to work with experienced professionals. Ensure that your employees are knowledgeable about the items and services you provide. This will also allow them to respond to client complaints more promptly and efficiently.

These are only a few of the most important elements in providing good customer service. If you want to keep your consumers happy and satisfied, be sure to prioritize these crucial areas. With so many factors to consider while running a business, try to make the customer experience as stress-free and pleasant as possible for your customers.

## Stories from the Field: Engaging Your Audience.

One of the most effective methods to captivate your audience is to narrate a story using field study data. Stories are effective tools for connecting with emotions, generating curiosity, and illustrating your views. To tell a tale, you must have a clear structure, an engaging narrative, and a significant message. Begin with a hook that captures their attention and introduces your main topic or concern. Then explain how you conducted your field study, what you discovered, and how you evaluated your results. Finally, include a conclusion that highlights your key takeaways and consequences.

# CHAPTER 8:

# SCALING YOUR BUSINESS: AND OUTSOURCING.

**What is Outsourcing?**

Outsourcing is the process of contracting someone outside of a corporation to execute services or generate things. In certain circumstances, things were formerly handled in-house by the company's own employees and staff. Outsourcing is a practice that businesses typically use to save money or as a strategic management tool. As a result, it can have an impact on a variety of vocations, including customer service, manufacturing, and back office operations.

Outsourcing became more popular as a corporate strategy in the 1990s, when multinational corporations outsourced logistics and manufacturing, among other activities. However, due to its broader economic repercussions, outsourcing is highly controversial in many countries. Opponents believe that it has resulted in the loss of domestic jobs, particularly in the industrial sector. Supporters argue that outsourcing encourages enterprises and firms to invest resources where they are most productive, and that it helps to preserve the character of free-market economies in an interconnected globe.

**KEY TAKEAWAYS**

Companies utilize outsourcing to reduce labor expenditures such as employee pay, overhead, equipment, and technology.

Companies employ outsourcing to focus on the core components of their business while offloading less vital processes to third-party groups.

On the negative side, communication between the organization and external providers can be difficult, and security risks may increase when numerous parties have access to critical data.

In some circumstances, businesses will outsource in order to shift things around on their balance sheet.

Outsourcing personnel, such as 1099 contract workers, can help the corporation pay taxes.

Understanding Outsourcing

When a corporation uses outsourcing, it hires outside organizations that are not linked with the company to accomplish specific duties. Outside organizations generally have different remuneration systems with their personnel than the outsourcing company, allowing them to execute the work for a lower cost. This finally allows the company that chose to outsource to reduce its labor expenditures by combining lower compensation with fewer benefits.

In addition to cost savings, outsourcing allows businesses to focus more on their core competencies. Outsourcing non-core activities can boost efficiency and production since another entity is better at these smaller jobs than the corporation. This method may also result in speedier turnaround times, enhanced competitiveness within an industry, and reduced overall operational expenses.

**Examples Of Outsourcing**

The primary benefits of outsourcing are reduced time and costs. A personal computer manufacturer may purchase internal components from other companies to reduce production costs. A law company may use a cloud-computing service provider to store and back up its files, allowing it to gain access to digital technology without having to invest substantial sums of money.

A small company may decide to outsource bookkeeping to an accounting firm since it is less expensive than hiring an in-house accountant. Other organizations benefit from outsourcing human resource department operations such as payroll and health insurance. When implemented correctly, outsourcing is an effective cost-cutting method that can even give a company a competitive advantage over its competitors.

**What are some criticisms of outsourcing?**
Outsourcing has downsides. For example, executing contracts with other companies may require more time and work from a company's legal team. Furthermore, security risks might

arise when another party has access to a company's personal information and experiences a data breach. Furthermore, there may be a breakdown in communication between the organization and the outsourced provider, which could cause project completion delays.

Aside from these factors, outsourcing has been criticized for job precarity and a lack of opportunity for contract workers to advance their careers. As previously stated, contract workers frequently earn less than full-time employees and receive fewer benefits, resulting in workplace disparities.

What Are the Benefits of Outsourcing Internationally?

Outsourcing globally can help businesses benefit from differences in labor and production costs between countries. Price disparities in another country may attract a company to shift some or all of its activities to the lower-cost country in order to boost profitability and remain competitive within an industry. Many multinational firms have eliminated their entire in-house customer support contact centers, outsourcing the role to third-party providers in lower-cost areas.

According to a Deloitte survey, the top three nations for outsourcing shared services in 2023 are India, Poland, and Mexico. Meanwhile, outsourcing IT service desk functions was the most popular service exported in the information technology sector worldwide.

## Using Technology for Growth

10 Ways Technology Can Help Your Growing Business
- Improved efficiency
- Enhanced Communications
- Better Data Management
- Adaptation and Flexibility
- Access to global markets.
- Quality Customer Service
- Cost Savings
- A competitive advantage.
- Scalability
- Risk Management

Technology's significant impact on business.

- **Improved efficiency**

Technology is critical to improving the efficiency of a developing organization. By automating tedious work and optimizing procedures, technology frees up your staff' time and energy for more strategic initiatives. For example, software solutions such as electrical contractor software CRM can automate billing, supply management, and customer service, eliminating the need for manual involvement and lowering the risk of errors. This not only speeds up task completion, but also provides improved precision and consistency, resulting in increased productivity and cost savings for the firm.

- **Enhanced Communications**

Effective communication is critical to the success of any business, particularly as it grows and expands. Technology offers a variety of tools and platforms that allow team members to communicate seamlessly, regardless of their location. Email, instant messaging, video conferencing, and collaborative software platforms allow employees to share information, collaborate on projects, and make real-time choices. This increases teamwork, promotes innovation, and guarantees that everyone is on the same page, resulting in increased productivity and cohesion within the firm.

- **Better Data Management**

In today's data-driven corporate environment, good data management is essential for making sound decisions and achieving a competitive advantage. Technology allows organizations to collect, store, and analyze massive volumes of data from a variety of sources, including consumer interactions, sales transactions, and market trends. Advanced analytics tools and software platforms enable businesses to gain important insights from their data, detecting patterns, trends, and opportunities that would otherwise go undiscovered. Businesses that use data effectively may streamline their operations, improve consumer experiences, and drive growth and innovation.

- **Adaptation and Flexibility**

Flexibility is critical for reacting to changing market conditions and meeting the demands of a developing firm. Technology provides the tools and infrastructure required to allow flexible work arrangements, such as remote working and flexible hours. Cloud computing, mobile devices, and collaborative tools allow employees to work from anywhere, at any time, without the need for a physical office. This not only enhances work-life balance and job happiness, but also enables organizations to tap into a global talent pool, scale operations more efficiently, and respond rapidly to new possibilities and problems.

- **Access to global markets.**

Technology has altered how organizations operate and connect with customers, creating new chances for growth and expansion in worldwide marketplaces. The Internet, e-commerce platforms, and digital marketing channels allow businesses to reach clients outside of their local markets and establish a global presence. With the correct IT infrastructure and digital strategy, firms can build an online presence, target certain demographics, and provide personalized experiences to clients all over the world. Access to global markets not only boosts revenue possibilities, but it also diversifies risk and lowers reliance on a particular market or location.

- **Quality Customer Service**

Providing outstanding customer service is critical for increasing customer loyalty and business growth. Technology improves the customer experience by allowing firms to provide quick, tailored, and efficient service through many channels. Chatbots and virtual assistants, for example, may handle routine inquiries and provide consumers with fast support, lowering wait times and increasing satisfaction. CRM software enables firms to track customer interactions, collect feedback, and discover areas for development. Businesses that use technology to provide exceptional customer service can differentiate themselves from competition, create strong relationships with customers, and promote long-term success.

- **Cost Savings**

Cost management is a top responsibility for developing firms, and technology provides several ways to cut costs and increase profitability. Technology enables businesses to run more efficiently and save waste by automating manual procedures, eliminating paper-based workflows, and optimizing resource allocation. For example, cloud computing enables organizations to extend their infrastructure on demand, paying only for the resources they use rather than investing in expensive hardware and maintenance. Similarly, software-as-a-service (SaaS) solutions provide subscription-based pricing structures that eliminate initial expenditures while lowering total cost of ownership. Businesses that use technology to reduce expenses and improve operational efficiency can better allocate resources, invest in growth projects, and remain competitive in the marketplace.

- **A competitive advantage.**

In today's fast-paced corporate world, staying ahead of the competition necessitates ongoing innovation and adaptation. Technology gives organizations the tools and capabilities they need to innovate faster, respond to market changes more effectively, and provide superior products and services to their consumers. For example, data analytics, artificial intelligence, and machine learning enable organizations to acquire deeper insights into customer preferences, market trends, and competitive dynamics, allowing them to anticipate customer wants and stay ahead of the competition. Businesses that embrace the newest technological trends and invest in digital transformation efforts can differentiate themselves from competitors, gain market share, and position themselves for long-term success.

Scalability

As businesses expand and adapt, they require IT solutions that can seamlessly scale to meet rising demands and complexity. Starting a small business or running a large enterprise necessitates technology that provides scalable infrastructure, software, and services that can scale with your company, allowing you to expand operations, enter new markets, and serve a larger customer base with minimal disruption or downtime. For example, cloud-based platforms provide almost limitless scalability, allowing firms to add or remove resources as needed to suit changing needs. Similarly, modular software architectures and open APIs allow organizations to rapidly integrate new capabilities and third-party services, ensuring that their technology stack stays agile and adaptive to changing business requirements. Businesses can use scalable technology solutions to future-proof their operations, reduce risk, and maintain agility in a fast changing business landscape.

- **Risk Management**

Cybersecurity threats and data breaches offer major dangers to businesses of all sizes, with the potential to cause financial losses, reputational damage, and legal penalties. Technology helps to mitigate these risks by implementing advanced security controls and compliance frameworks that safeguard sensitive data and systems from unauthorized access, theft, and hostile assaults. Encryption technologies, multi-factor authentication, and intrusion detection systems are all used to protect data and prevent illegal access to networks and applications. Compliance management tools and risk assessment frameworks help firms discover and handle potential risks, ensuring they follow industry rules and best practices. Businesses may secure their assets, develop consumer trust, and maintain their marketplace reputation by prioritizing cybersecurity and investing in comprehensive risk management practices.

- **Technology's significant impact on business.**

Finally, technology has a significant impact on the success trajectory of a growing organization. Businesses that embrace innovation and use the right technological solutions can improve efficiency, streamline processes, and create new chances for development and expansion. Technology has numerous and far-reaching benefits, including improved communication and cooperation, data-driven decision-making, and risk mitigation. As firms manage the intricacies of a quickly changing business landscape, integrating technology becomes a strategic essential for keeping ahead of the competition and achieving long-term success. By leveraging technology, organizations can future-proof their operations, generate innovation, and survive in an increasingly digital world.

## Entrepreneur Journeys: Successful Scaling Up.

The Four Major Stages of the Entrepreneurial Journey

- Execute: Starting a business necessitates a leap of faith and an openness to taking risks.
  To get started, entrepreneurs must execute their ideas precisely and quickly.
  This entails responding rapidly to changing market conditions, making sound financial decisions, and laying a solid platform for future expansion.
- Completing the implementation phase of entrepreneurship can be a demanding endeavor, requiring a great deal of attention and effort.
  One of the most difficult challenges entrepreneurs face during this stage is adapting to changing market conditions.
  To remain competitive in an ever-changing business environment, entrepreneurs must be able to adapt their strategies and tactics.
  This necessitates a willingness to take chances and make difficult judgments, frequently with incomplete knowledge.
- Furthermore, entrepreneurs must be able to make sound financial decisions in order

to secure the long-term viability of their company. This can include managing cash flow, investing wisely, and striking a balance between short-term and long-term goals.
- Finally, entrepreneurs must lay a solid basis for future growth by implementing effective processes and procedures, recruiting the right people, and fostering an environment of innovation and cooperation.

By overcoming these obstacles and executing their ideas with precision and agility, entrepreneurs can position themselves for long-term success in their quest to build a successful business.

I've realized that systematizing my operations is a necessary step in achieving my objectives. It's been a difficult journey, but I believe I'm now in the right place.

Adapting my processes to accommodate growth has been one of my most tough challenges. I had to develop and implement procedures that could be scaled across departments and locations while maintaining quality and efficiency.

It's been a difficult balancing act, requiring me to constantly evaluate and adjust my systems to ensure they remain effective. Additionally, I've had to delegate responsibilities to others while maintaining a consistent level of quality. This has required a high level of trust and communication and the ability to train and mentor employees effectively.

Finally, I've had to make difficult decisions about which systems and processes to prioritize, as resources are frequently limited in the early stages of growth. However, by persevering in the face of adversity, I am building a successful business with the potential for long-term growth and success.

Scrutinize: To stay competitive in today's environment, firms must constantly analyze their operations and look for ways to improve. This entails assessing data, monitoring key performance indicators, and identifying opportunities for optimization.

By scrutinizing their business, entrepreneurs can make informed decisions and stay ahead of the curve.

Finally, every entrepreneur must eventually leave their business. This could include selling the business, handing it down to the next generation, or simply moving on to new opportunities.

Entrepreneurs who plan for an exit from the start can build a valuable business that can be sold for a high price and leave a lasting legacy.

**So, where are you?**

**To determine which stage you are currently in on your entrepreneurial journey, try the following actionable steps:**

**Execute:** Consider whether you have taken the necessary risk in starting your business. Do you make sound financial judgments and adjust to changing market conditions? Have you constructed a stable foundation for future growth?

**Systematize:** Have you built scalable processes and procedures that can be copied across numerous departments and locations? Are you able to distribute responsibility to others while keeping a constant level of quality?

**Examine:** Do you regularly analyze data, track key performance indicators, and identify opportunities for improvement? Do you make informed decisions to stay ahead of the curve?

**Exit:** Have you considered your long-term business goals? Are you preparing for an eventual exit, whether by selling the company, passing it down to the next generation, or moving on to new ventures?

Answering these questions honestly helps me understand where I am in my entrepreneurial journey and what steps I need to take to achieve my objectives. How about you?

I was happy to share this, and I hope it encourages some excellent talks. I'd love to hear from you if you're working on putting this into action or have already gone through that stage. Feedback is always appreciated, especially as we continue to develop and refine our approach.

# CHAPTER 9:

# MAINTAINING LONG-TERM SUCCESS BY STAYING CURRENT WITH INDUSTRY TRENDS

**10 Tips for Staying On Top of Trends**

Most individuals think about the future when they celebrate the New Year. However, as entrepreneurs, we should be thinking about the future all year round. Staying up to date on trends that affect your organization, your customers, and your industry is critical to maintaining your competitiveness.

Here are ten pointers for keeping up with trends.

Read voraciously. Read everything you can about your industry, market, and the world at large. Keep up with industry trade publications and websites; national, regional, and local media; notable bloggers, and business thought leaders.

Become involved in your industry. Join industry associations, attend events, receive training, and participate in online communities. Associations work hard to keep their members informed about trends, so take advantage of their knowledge.

Network. Get to know people in your field and beyond it. Regularly meet with coworkers, partners, and clients to discuss business developments. These discussions are sure to generate ideas.

- Stay in touch with your customers. Social networking platforms such as Facebook, LinkedIn, and Twitter make it easier than ever to learn what your customers think and want. Are they staying at home more? Spending less? Cooking more? All you need to do is ask.
- Keep track of your business. Financial predictions and company dashboards are useful tools for identifying trends and measuring corporate benchmarks. What things are selling and which aren't? Are the supply costs rising or falling? Tracking trends throughout time allows you to forecast prospective problems—and possibilities.

- Study statistics. Government organizations produce massive amounts of data that can help you identify patterns in demographic groupings, geographies, sectors, and more. The National Bureau of Economic Research, the United States Census Bureau, and Fedstats websites are excellent places to start.
- Examine your competition. Visit their locations and websites, and follow them on Facebook and Twitter. What new initiatives, goods, or services will they launch? Are they pursuing new markets or growing into other regions?
- Get out of the office. Regularly visit where your customers congregate--whether it's the neighborhood restaurant row, mall, or office park--and study what they're doing, wearing, and purchasing.
- Think outside the box. Look beyond your own sector, market, and location to see what people in unrelated fields are doing. Read the news from Japan or New York City. Visit websites for skateboarders or commodity dealers. Learning about trends

in other "worlds" will inspire you to create new ones of your own.
- Think long-term. Fads and trends are not the same thing, so don't get caught up in "what's hot now." Consider how a current trend will affect your industry in one, five, or ten years from now.

## Continuous Learning and Improvement.

What is continuous learning?

Continuous learning refers to the continuing expansion of knowledge and skill sets. Professional development in the workplace focuses on learning new skills and information while reinforcing what has already been mastered.

The definition of continuous learning is broad; it can be formal or informal, structured or unstructured in nature. Taking a formal course, observing more experienced employees, asking for help with an unfamiliar issue, exploring new and alternative work techniques, studying, conversing casually, and practicing the usage of a skill are all possible activities.

Daily habits and practices serve as the foundation for continual learning. This form of learning can occur through any method of knowledge acquisition and can continue throughout one's lifetime.

Continuous learning programs in the workplace can boost employee engagement, job happiness, and knowledge retention. To be competitive, firms must constantly adapt to changing social and economic conditions. Because an organization's success is dependent on its people, it is critical that employee skill sets grow to match the demands of the business environment. Continuous learning is one approach to accomplish this.

**Principles of Continuous Learning**

In traditional employee training, the amount of employee knowledge reaches a high immediately following a given training course or event, then steadily declines over time due to lack of reinforcement. Employees retain knowledge more effectively when they participate in many learning activities that reinforce one another.

The goal of continuous learning in the workplace is for people to retain their knowledge and abilities over time. Reinforcement exercises help employees gain more knowledge and keep it for longer periods of time.

**Some critical components are required to provide a continuous learning environment. They include the following:**

Learning possibilities are easily accessible anytime needed.

Learners get continuous opportunities to apply their knowledge and put their new skills to the test.

A culture that encourages learning through sustainable behaviors that can be successfully replicated.

Opportunities for collaboration allow learners to share their expertise and viewpoints.

Regular feedback systems for both instructors and students.

Benefits of Continuous Learning

Continuous learning in the workplace has the ability to broaden employee skills, promote knowledge and skill retention, develop new ideas and views, boost morale, and improve overall employee performance.

Individual employees gain from continual learning in a variety of ways, including

Assists them in achieving their professional development goals.
Allows them to earn or upgrade professional licenses and certificates.
Encourages people to pursue new chances and views in their professional and personal development.
Allows people to acquire marketable professional abilities through upskilling and reskilling.
Continuous learning has other benefits for the organization, such as:
Contributes to accomplishing corporate objectives.
Encourages a forward-thinking, innovative culture.
Makes employees feel valued.
Cost savings are achieved by investing in the continued development of current personnel rather than training new employees.

Increases competitiveness as employees become more skilled and productive.

**Continuous Learning Modeling**

Deloitte's Continuous Learning Model includes the following considerations:

According to the Deloitte approach, learners' demands can be divided into three categories:

Immediate. Learning is necessary for success today.

Intermediate. Learning required to broaden skill sets and advance in present roles.

Transitional. Learning required to achieve long-term company objectives, advance up the career ladder, or make a career change.

**Paradigms are the various ways that employees learn.**

**They contain the following:**

- Education. This is traditional learning and development, which is typically done in classrooms or through e-learning experiences. This form of learning is often trackable and has a distinct beginning and end.
- Experience. This involves learning through workplace events such as special

initiatives, job rotations, and stretch assignments.
- Exposure. This type of learning occurs as a result of social interactions.
- Environment. This includes the tools and procedures that help employees learn inStrategies for continuous learning

**The strategies that use continuous learning techniques include the following:**
- Structured learning. These are structured learning approaches designed for certain goals and purposes. They consist of school courses, online learning courses, workshops, seminars, webinars, conferences, and employee and managerial training programs.
- Social learning. This refers to the methods in which people learn by engaging and observing others. It might be professional or informal, in-person or via virtual channels. Discussion, coworking, collaborative problem solving, mentoring, and on-the-job training are examples of social learning activities.

- Self-directed learning. These are self-administered measurements that employees can use to improve their skills and knowledge. This form of learning might occur randomly or on a set schedule. It entails study, reading, experimentation, and practice testing.

How to Create a Continuous Learning Strategy

A continuous learning approach begins with business leaders or individuals in charge of employee training defining long-term learning objectives. Then, a learning infrastructure is put in place, which comprises a variety of courses and tools to help reach those objectives.

Organizations must foster a supportive continuous learning environment, as employees who are focused on reaching urgent job deadlines may be hesitant to take on new learning opportunities.

**Business executives can take the following steps to promote continual learning:**
- Begin with a plan. By outlining a plan of action, you can demonstrate to employees that your firm is spending time and resources in continuous learning. This

should include areas where learning strategies are implemented, such as for individual employees, teams, departments, and the entire business. Management and staff should communicate to clarify objectives and priorities.
- Leadership. A continual learning culture begins at the top. That is why it is critical for management to express their complete support for these initiatives.
- Creating a culture of constant learning.
  Once the scope of a continuous learning strategy has been identified and a plan developed, the following stages will ensure that employees may fully utilize it in their work environment:
- Flexibility when implementing learning plans. Flexibility is essential for accommodating as many employees as possible while assuring their participation. Flexible ways include giving workers enough time to finish assignments while taking into account their busy schedules and personal life. Another example would be easily available forums or discussion

boards for remote learners to collaborate and interact.
- Effective technological tools and resources. LMS software is very useful for cohort learning, which involves training or educating several employees at the same time. Systems that provide virtual and hybrid learning are also important.
- Collaborative and collaborative learning initiatives. LMSes can promote cooperation and interactive assignments through features such as forums and gamification. When students engage in enjoyable activities and relationships, they are more likely to remember what they are learning.

**Continuous learning for AI and ML**

Continuous learning is a notion that applies to both artificial intelligence (AI) and machine learning (ML). Ongoing learning is an essential component of these systems. ML systems employ algorithms to learn how to evaluate data on their own. Algorithms assist them in identifying key insights and determining what forecasts can be made based on that information.

In a static learning process, once an ML algorithm has been trained on a certain data set, it expects that any subsequent data sets it analyzes will be similar. However, neither the world nor knowledge are static. As a result, much as humans must be retrained and reskilled through continual learning, ML systems require continuous training as part of the ML operations process.

An ML model is deployed once, then continuously monitored and retrained to respond to ever-changing data. Developers in this industry employ a variety of strategies and tools to automate the retraining process.

A human developer must monitor the continuous learning process for ML on a regular basis. This sort of retraining also has limitations, such as the need for expensive technical infrastructures and the time-consuming nature of the procedure. However, continuous learning is required to ensure the effectiveness of AI and ML systems.

# Personal Accounts: Staying ahead and innovating.

The Need for Strategic Innovation

Innovation, at its core, is about discovering innovative solutions to problems or capitalizing on emerging trends and technologies. However, strategic innovation extends beyond brief bursts of brilliance. It entails a systematic strategy to identify, develop, and implement new ideas that are consistent with your company's long-term objectives and competitive advantage.

**Understanding the Competitive Landscape.**

Before entering into strategic innovation, it is critical to understand the competitive environment. In today's global market, competitors might appear from unexpected places, and customer preferences can shift in the blink of an eye. To stay ahead, business owners must constantly analyze their competitors, industry developments, and consumer behavior.

**The Process of Strategic Innovation**

**Market Research:** Begin by gathering information and insights about your industry, competitors, and intended audience. Understand their concerns, needs, and preferences.

**Idea Generation:** Encourage innovation among your team members. Generate ideas for addressing identified difficulties or capitalizing on upcoming possibilities.

**Idea Screening:** Not all ideas are the same. Evaluate each concept in terms of feasibility, alignment with your business strategy, and potential influence on your market position.

Prototyping and Testing: Create prototypes or minimal viable products (MVPs) to test the most promising concepts. Collect feedback from customers or focus groups to improve your concepts.

**Implementation:** After you have validated an idea, create a detailed implementation strategy. This could include modifications to your products, services, procedures, or business strategy.

**Continuous improvement:** Innovation is an ongoing process. Regularly assess and enhance your innovations in response to feedback and changing market conditions.

Creating an innovative culture.

Strategic innovation should be integrated in your organization's culture rather than being only the job of a few individuals. Encourage your team members to communicate openly, share ideas, and experiment together. Reward and recognise original thinking, even if some ideas might not provide instant results. Remember that failures can provide excellent learning opportunities.

**Measuring the Impact**
To assess the success of your strategic innovation activities, set key performance indicators (KPIs) that are aligned with your business objectives. These could include increased market share, enhanced customer happiness, or greater profitability. Regularly evaluate your success and alter your strategy as appropriate.

Strategic innovation is no longer a luxury in today's hyper-competitive business environment; it is a requirement. It is the driving force behind remaining relevant, seizing opportunities, and retaining a competitive advantage. Embrace an innovative culture, keep an eye on your industry, and be ready to adapt and change. This allows you to establish your company as a market leader, resulting in long-term success and expansion.

# Conclusion:

## Your Roadmap to Success

As we conclude this journey of developing your internet empire, it's time to reflect on everything you've learned. This book has walked you through the necessary stages for recognizing your unique skills and developing them into a profitable business. From developing a clear foundation to managing marketing and producing money, each chapter provides practical tips to help you negotiate the internet world.

In this final section, we'll review the key points from each chapter. Consider it a fast refresher of the previously described tactics and ideas. We'll also share some encouraging words, reminding you that, while the road ahead may be difficult, it is also full of chances.

Your adventure does not finish here; it is only the beginning. The path to success is constantly shifting, so it's critical to be curious, adaptable, and committed to your goals. Remember, the world of internet business is vast and ever-changing, but with the appropriate mindset and tools, you can confidently face any challenge and achieve your goals.

Thank you for joining us on this adventure. Best wishes as you continue to grow and thrive!

**Please leave a honest review if you find this book helpful**

www.ingramcontent.com/pod-product-compliance
Lightning Source LLC
Chambersburg PA
CBHW071916210526
45479CB00002B/435